THE

MONOLO

REAYA SEALEY

ADRIANA
HAPPY BIRTHDAY 2021
X MAN

ISBN: 978-1-5272-8698-6

Poco,

Missy, Jev,

Jani, Daigon, Kyson

FOREWORD

Back in 2010, I was walking into work on a Saturday for another day of auditions. A young woman walking in front of me caught my eye, she was trotting along at a pace, trundling a small suitcase behind her. She looked so purposeful. I thought; I do hope she is heading in to audition for the acting course, and lo and behold 30 minutes later, there she was on the front row of the movement class with this fierce determination on her face. She was committed to getting into the school! Fast-forward 3 years to Graduate Showcase and looking for suitable monologues.

We had a clear idea of what we were looking for but struggled to find many monologues in a Jamaican accent, let alone having sufficient choice to find the right speech for Reaya.

Fast forward again and I receive an email from Reaya asking if I wouldn't mind looking at a manuscript of speeches she had written. I was so impressed with the quality and authenticity of the voices. This manuscript provides a much-needed resource for actors, student actors, and anybody who is interested in working in authentic Jamaican dialect. With ever-increasing interest in stories and content other than from within the European paradigm, this is a timely addition to the canon of monologue anthologies.

I look forward to seeing how this material will support the next generation of determined young actors as they rock up to auditions and place themselves in the front row, determined to get that role!

Danièle Sanderson
Head of UG Studies – Acting
Royal Birmingham Conservatoire

Growing up in Birmingham, life was full of Jamican culture. Music, Clothes, Food, Language, everything was different. At school they spoke differently, at home it wasn't the same...I had no idea what Cockles or Toad in the Hole was, nor did they understand what Ital food, Rice and Peas, and Jumbo steak cuisine was. At School I learnt about The Big Bang, Spice Girls and Upside the Head, meanwhile at home we played Brown Girl in the Ring, learnt about Haille Salassie and Nanny and the Maroons whilst trickles of rocksteady, reggae and dub echoed in the background.

As an Actor searching for Black Monologues in Drama School proved difficult, they were far and few between and they weren't even Jamaican Monologues I had been searching for at the time. With Jamaican and African ethnicity combined with English Nationality I think this is a very important aspect of monologues which is missing from our repertoire. I think it's important to have access to these types of Monologues and not allow

Jamaican Patois to slip through the cracks of our industry, we must keep it alive, especially considering we are hearing splashes of the dialect within different media platforms.

My reasons behind writing this book are quite precise. There are no other Patois books to support Jamaican speaking Actors who intend to learn or audition for a Jamaican speaking role, irrespective of their ethnicity.

CONTENTS

ACKNOWLEDGMENTS

Amanda Huxtable. Annika Allan. Chirag Lukha. Claire Simpson. Everal A Walsh. Flo Wilson. Hamish Glen.Jade Samuels.Justine Themen. Judith Jacob. Lizzie Adejemi. Obidaya. Ola Animashawun. Roshida Mcogg. Ruksanna Fernandez.Sharon D Clarke MBE. Shirley Harris. Simon Ratcliffe. Samir Bhamra. Sonja Smith. Tanya Gasa. Titilola Dawudu. Vivianne Sengati. Vontesse Betson.

Online Book Launch- 9th April 2021- Pre recorded filmed, audio and animation created and performed by Amanda Huxtable, Everal Walsh, Flo Wilson, Judith Jacob, Jade Samuels, Sharon D Clarke MBE and Vanitas arts.

Days Of Our Lives

1960. Jamaica.

Aunty, 60s. Wears a white frock, head scarf with bare feet. She is short and has a little frame, but by looking at her you will know not to mess with Aunty. Even though her frame is small, her hands are wide and "tick". Aunty sits on the Veranda which is yet to be complete. It has the front but the sides are yet to be built. Aunty has received a letter from her niece who is abroad. Aunty tells her son Ezekiel, who is currently climbing a tree for the lizard which had just escaped from the grip of his hands, to come and listen to her read the letter. Laba Laba tends not to engage when his mother receives the letters. It reminds him that he is alone and his closest cousin has migrated, but unbeknownst to his Mother, he takes in every word even though each syllable spoken feels like daggers to his heart. She begins to read the letter and interjects now and then by making comments to Laba Laba and herself.

See di letter ere. Come dung from deh. Yuh know seh yuh can't duh two tings one time, an a one time mi a read it suh nuh badda preten cork up yuh ears...Ow it write suh?

Irie Aunty, wah gwarn Laba Laba!

She a arsk yuh wah gwarn Ezekiel.

The letter nuh write too good Aunty. Yuh always tell me "whatever sweet yuh gwein sour yuh"...But mi did a teef out likkle food outa di Dutchi and bun up mi finger pon it.

It fi get chop off.

Daddy spray suhum yellow an put plaster pon it, dat a why my writing crabby suh, an di likkle grease yuh see pon di envelope a from Nagina, she did a farse wid it when we a eat wi food, come grease it up wid ar narsty finger dem.

Woo! Nagina always a fars wid someting.

Is Daddy bring Fish and Chip fi wi dinner. Wi eat it pon Friday evening, im bring it when him dun work. Wi nuh ave nuttun like it back home. Chip in a newspaper, yuh eva imagine dat?

Is weh she a talk bout, food inna paper?

But it taste good, mi like it wid di salt and vinegar. Laba Laba wouldn't like it wid di salt and vinegar pon it, yuh know ow im like im food dry.

Yuh ear weh she seh Laba Laba, she seh yuh dry like. (Laughs) From mi born an grow, mi neva yet ear bout eat food outa newspaper. A muss Hinglish ting dat.

Is Mummy and Daddy turn fi host party again tonight. Mi hear seh is Mr Thomas tomorrow but mi neva ketch a who a host pon Sunday. Last time wi sit pon top a di stairs a listen music an a dance and wi hear Daddy a cuss out Mr

Banks cah him a try rub-a-dub wid one woman but she neva want dance..
Mi arsk Daddy bout it

Jheeze-u-wiz. Lord dis yah gyal bright ec.

Me asrk Daddy bout it but him tell mi fi guh bout mi business an kibber mi mout. But yuh couldn't guess an tell me a who di woman be? Nuh Blundell from back a wi. Me nayn know she did come a England.

Me nayn know neida mi love.

Is only likkle while we deh over her but it feel like years since wi nuh see unuh.
Me miss Jamaica bad. Dung tuh di smell, England don't smell like Jamaica yuh know, me can't believe it. How peculiar.

Hear ar bout perculiar, she sound British tuh backside.

Tuesdeh Mawnin wi wake fi gah school and when we open up di curtain, pure white outside. We fright yuh si. We arsk Momma weh it be an she seh it call SINOW. Wi never yet have SINOW in Jamaica.
When we walk gah school di sinow tall yuh see, it cover wi knee when we a walk an by time school dun wi foot cole and wet, but Daddy seh we a fi wear two socks till we get we new shoes.
School a nuh like back ome...No Anansi stories or nuh un like dat.

Eh eh!

Weh no black no dog no Irish mean? Me see it pon one window when we a guh Market. Me arsk Mommy weh it mean but she tell me fi hush and draw me weh. All now she nuh answer me.

Lord Jesus.

She seh di barrel sen and it soon reach now. How everyting back home? Me hear seh unuh under curfew again, everybody alright? Me ongle ere wah pun when big people a talk, suh me nuh know wah gwarn too tough.

Yuh fi glad yuh deh a Hingland girl chile.

Me long fi see unuh, but Daddy seh yuh nah come over, but yuh tell me seh a di paper dem yuh a wait pon. A trut him a talk Aunty?

(Kisses teeth) Chu! Weh im open up im mout fa?

Suh me nah guh see yuh and Ezekiel again?
Fi now, or fi ever...me nuh know which.
Me tun mi back.

Dumplin.
(Calls to Ezekiel) Laba Laba, run guh get me one pencil and one piece a paper...Eh bwoy! Nuh badda mek I spit dry before yuh come.

Translation

Here's the letter. Get down from there. You know that you can't do two things at the same time and I'm only going to read it once so don't bother pretending you're not listening. Why is it written like this?

Hello Auntie, what's happening Laba Laba?

She's asking how you are Laba Laba.

The letter isn't written well auntie. You always tell me "whatever sweets me is going to sour me", but I stole some food out of the Dutch pot and burnt my finger on it.

It should have gotten chopped off.

Daddy sprayed something yellow and put a plaster on it, that's why my handwriting's a little bit shabby, and the oil on the envelope is from Nagina.

She was messing with it when we were eating our food. Came and greased it up with their sticky fingers.

Wooy! Nagina's always messing with something.

Daddy brought us fish and chips for dinner. We have it on Friday evenings, he brings it when he comes home from work. We don't have anything like that back home. Chips in the newspaper, could you ever imagine that?

What is she talking about, food in paper?

But it tastes good, I like it with salt and vinegar. Laba Laba wouldn't like it with salt and vinegar on it, You know how he likes his food dry.

Did you hear what she said Laba Laba? She said you're dry like.
(Laughs)

Since I've been born I've never heard about eating food out of newspaper. That must be an English thing.

It's Mummy and Daddy's turn to host a party again tonight. I heard it's Mr Thomas's tomorrow, but I didn't hear who is going to host it on Sunday.
Last time we sat on top of the stairs listening to the music and dancing and we heard Daddy shouting at Mr Banks because he tried to Dance with a woman, but she didn't want to. I asked daddy about it.

Jheeze you wizz. Lord this girl is forward.

I asked daddy about it and he told me to go about my business and keep my mouth shut.

Guess who the woman was? It was Blundell from behind where we live. I didn't know she came to England.

I didn't know either my love.

We've only been over here for a little while, but it feels like years since I've seen youse. I miss Jamaica bad. Even down to the smell, England doesn't smell like Jamaica. I can't believe it. How peculiar.

Listen to her, about 'peculiar'.

She does sound British.

On Tuesday morning we woke up to go to school and when we opened the curtains it was just white outside. We were a little frightened. We asked mama what it was and she said it was called snow. We've never had snow in Jamaica before. When we walked to school the snow was so high, it covered our knees when we walked and by the time we finished school, our feet were cold and wet, but Daddy said we have to wear two pairs of socks until we get our new shoes. School is not like back home. No Anancy stories or nothing like that.

Oh wow.

What does no black no dog No Irish mean? I saw it on the window when we were going to the market. I asked Mommy what it meant, but she told me to be quiet and pulled me away. She still hasn't answered me.

Lord Jesus.

She said the barrels sent and it should reach you soon. How's everything back home? I heard you guys are under curfew again, is everybody alright?

I only hear what's happening when big people are talking, so I don't know what's happening really.

You should be glad you're in England girl child.

I long to see you, but daddy said you're not coming over, but you told me that you were waiting for your papers. Is he telling the truth Aunty? (kisses teeth?)

Damn. What did he open his mouth for?

So I'm not going to see you and Ezekiel again?

For now or forever, I don't know which.

See you soon

Dumpling.

(Calls to Ezekiel)

Laba Laba, go and get me a pencil and a piece of paper. Hey boy! Don't let my spit dry before you come back.

Presentable

Tamisha, 14 is at school. She has just been reprimanded for her hairstyle and told to leave the class and not return until it's at the schools standards. She had come back from seeing her family in Jamaica on the weekend and it's her first day back since her return. Her parents had paid for her hairdo whilst she was away. She wears her School uniform with her bag on her back and coat in her hands. Tamisha thinks she’s getting targeted because her hair is different. She makes a point to say her hair doesn't define her potential in the classroom, so it shouldn't have an effect on the teacher. She's upset and unsure what to do. She’s been in the toilets for around 4 minutes now. The toilets are old and cold. The doors of the cubicles are full of graffiti and with the windows being open, each squeak when they move, making it sound like a discordant orchestra of metal chairs being dragged across a wooden floor. A girl she knows comes in to use the toilet, but truthfully, she has just used it as an excuse to get out of her French lesson. She asks her what's wrong, comforts her and offers her some Nerds...

Him tell me fi stan up a di front a di class-Me did tink seh im did a guh praise me fi mi homework weh me do b'cah yuh know seh mi work always good-An yuh dun know how mi Fada stay wid mi homework already. Suh Mr Blakely ask me if me tink me dress correctly fi school, me tell im yes, of course. Me ask im if him tink mi Mada an Fada a guh alow me fi come out a di yard dress like tramp. Suh me ask im weh wrong wid how me dress b'cah a di sed uniform me wear gah school all di time. Den di faisty man tun round an ask me, weh dat in a mi ead?-Not, why yuh have beads in yuh air? Or, why dem suh colourful?-Weh dat in a yuh ead?-Me tell im is air beads me ave in deh. Me ask im if him cyar see good mek im a fi a ask me idiot question suh, im cuss me, tell me fi tek dem out an don't return till me do it...Tek it out fi wah? Is him mention seh it dangerous, it only dangerous if sombady fars wid it or chry tek it out. A nearly tree hour me sidung fi get mi head plat up, an him wah come tell me fi tek it out because him seh it inappropriate? Yuh know ow much money mi Mada an Fada spen pan dis fi mek sure mi head pretty fi school?

Now him wah tell me fi eida tek it out an walk roun school wid bedraggle air, or guh home an miss mi education fi di res a di day...Suh weh me fi do?

Me cyar tek dem out b'cah me a guh get cuss, an me cyar guh ome b'cah nuhbady nuh deh deh...See ow him stay dough? It nuh seh nuttun in di uniform section bout ave bead in a yuh ead, chry mek up rule as dem feel.

Translation

He told me to stand up in front of the class-I thought he was going to praise me for the homework I had done, because you know my work's always good-And you know what my Fathers like with my homework. So, Mr Blakely asked me if I thought I was dressed Correctly for school, I told him yes, of course. I asked him if he thinks my parents are going to allow me to come out dressed like a tramp. I asked him what was wrong with how I'm dressed because it's the same uniform I wear for school all the time. Then the cheeky man turned around and asked me what that was in my hair?-Not, why do you have beads in your hair? Or, why are they so colourful?-What's that in your hair?-I told him I have hair beads in there. I asked him if he can't see very well, because of the idiotic question he asked, he shouted at me, told me to take them out and not to return until I do it...Take it out for what? He mentioned that it was dangerous, it's only dangerous if somebody messes with it or tries to take it out. I sat down for nearly 3 hours getting my hair plaited and he wants to come and tell me to take it out because he says it's inappropriate? Do you know how much money my parents spent on this to make sure my hair is pretty for school? Now he's telling me to either take it out and walk around school with my bedraggled hair, or go home and miss my education for the rest of the day...So what am I supposed to do? I can't take them out because they're going to shout and I can't go home because nobodys there...See what he's like? It doesn't say anything in the uniform section about having beads in your hair, they make up rules as they feel like it.

Once A Man, Twice A Child

Grandad, 73

Late 1980s. He wears black trousers, a Jumper, a suit Jacket and slippers. It's early Autumn and the air is still, the leaves on the trees are beginning to change colour. The late afternoon is creeping into the evening. It's cold outside but inside it's nice and warm from the calogas as it radiates the room from burning on a low heat. The room has floral sofas, floral wallpaper and floral curtains; each of various colours and sizes. The furniture in the living room is of dark brown wood. There are family photos, mainly in black and white dotted around the space, frames nailed together as if the photographs are airborne, so as not to allow the image's to escape. On the table beside where Grandad sits in his chair, which the Grandchildren refer to as 'The Throne,' is a cup of half drunken English Tea and a half eaten slice of Toto. The horse racing is showing on the tv in the background but is on mute. Grandad is cleaning his records and playing them on his Gram to see how they sound. He sometimes cusses his Wife under his breath when the record jumps, as she tends to clean a lot and blames her for moving them, resulting in them being scratched...His Grandson has come to visit and has just informed his Grandfather that he is going to become a Great Grandfather. He tells his Grandfather that he will be working part time to spend as much time as he can with his son as he feels like he lost out when he was growing up due to his parents working all the time.

Yuh feel seh you a Man now? Wait till yuh pikni born. Nuh more a dem Chapparetta an colour colour crep weh you a buy. Back ome when we did a grow, we nyam weh put in front a wi-Mek my Mada ear talk bout me nuh wah dis, one box yuh get! Di likkle food weh feed di ten a wi a yard, cyar feed tree a unuh tideh di way uh nuh craven suh. Dem eat outa road till dem belly bang, dem nuh know weh dem a eat, bout chi-nee fi dinna. Yuh know seh people chop up darg an cook?-Nuh wonda di NHS strech out suh. Yuh granny chry ard fi mek sure we eat same way wi would a eat back a Jamaica. Rice an peas pan Sundeh, Satideh soup, Tuesdeh a tripe, yuh see weh me mean? Unuh lucky uh nuh ave school fi guh. Di likkle heducation me get a from mi Sista, an she get ar heducation from ar frien Celesteen when she use tuh visit ar Granny a holiday time. If she neva learn ar book me would neva able fi write mi name pan mi document when me ready fi chravel a forign. When we step foot pan Hinglish territory, we work everyday till wi ready fi retire-A nuh like today when uh nuh call uh nuh boss a seh mi belly a ot me, me nuh feel too good. Un nuh ave it good...Yuh tink Granny did talk suh when she back a yard? No sah! One heavnin me come in from work an all me ear a Be-ef!, Be-ef! When me guh in a di back room, me see ar a sidung in front a di radio wid one piece a paper an pencil a write dong Be-ef, suh dat when she guh a market she soun like she heducated an nuh jus come from forign. Yuh see weh we go trough fi yuh, fi mek sure you get beta life? Mek sure you duh di siam fi yuh pikni. Is a new season fi you now.

Beat

Congratulations mi bwoi!

Translation

You think you're a man now? Wait till your child's born. No more of those chapperettas and colorful trainers that you always buy.
Back home when we were growing up, we ate what was put in front of us-if my Mother heard, I don't want this, one box you get! The little bit of food which fed the ten of us at home, couldn't feed three of you today, the way you guys are so greedy. They eat at restaurants till their stomachs are full, they don't know what they are eating, about Chinese for dinner. Do you know that people chop up dogs and cook?-No wonder the NHS is under so much strain. Your grandmother tried hard to make sure we ate

the same way we would have eaten back in Jamaica. Rice and peas on Sunday, Saturday soup, Tuesday we ate tripe, do you see what I mean? You're lucky that you had a school to go to, the little bit of education I got was from my sister, and she got her education from her friend Celesteen when she used to visit her Granny in the School holidays. If she didn't learn her books, I would never have been able to write my name on my documents when I was ready to travel to England. When we stepped foot on English territory, we worked every day until we retired-It's not like today when you guys call your boss and say I've got a stomach ache, I don't feel too good. You guys have got it easy. Do you think Granny spoke like that when she was back home? No way!

One evening I came in from work and all I could hear was Be-ef! Be-ef! When I went into the back room, I saw her sitting in front of the radio with a piece of paper and pencil writing down Beef, so that when she goes down to the market she sounds like she's educated and not just coming from foreign.

Do you see what we went through for you, to make sure you get a better life? Make sure you do the same for your child. It's a new season for you now.

Beat

Congratulations my boy!

Zelfa, a tall, medium built woman in her 60s. She wears a long skirt, blouse and shoes with a very low heel. It's 1982, Newham, England. She stands in her living room, decorated in 1960s british decor with splashes of Jamaican culture. The rain drizzles on the window panes. Inside is warm but her son hasn't taken his coat off since he arrived, quite some time ago. Her son has decided to hear his mother out and confront her about his upbringing. She explains her reasons behind the decisions she made throughout her life and her feelings towards him. She sees herself as a champion in her career but a failure as Mother to her eldest son. They don't see each other very often due to a variety of issues. Due to that, they have grown apart and know very little about each other. Even though this is her home, she feels extremely uncomfortable, she doesn't know where to place herself. She wants forgiveness for what she has done but first she needs to explain once and for all. She's solemn. She says her peace and waits for him to make a move.

Me sign up fi di Army back ome, not in England. Me volenteer in Jamaica, an not long afta me complete di trainin me come a di UK. Me did a fi leave yuh wid Granny, an stay rest assured she tek care of yuh an bring yuh up in di correc mana, how my sibling an I did raise. She do dat an more. Me did wah carry yuh-Me would a carry yuh wid me, but me did ave nobody fi tek care a yuh when me deya work. Dat a di only option weh did viable at de time. Whole heap a people immigrate, lef dem Famliy fi guh wuk a forign all di time, yuh feel seh yuh a di firs fi get lef behin? If yuh did in a my position yuh would duh di same dont? A jus suh it guh, b'cah nuh big money a mek in a Jamaica...Den when me wed an have di twins, me did think is a good time fi bring yuh ova Agustus. Me mek plans fi sen yuh a school fi di las few years a yuh school heducation, fi yuh fi mek someting great fi yuhself.

Den ova time, Martin resent di taught a lovin sombody else chile, dat a di reason why we divorce. Den ave tuh restart ova again wid di two pikni dem. A long time it tek fi sort out tings. Me nayn a sen fi yuh an bring yuh in a chaos when yuh dun sekkle back ome. Me did a fi mek sure tings in arda fi yuh fi flourish in a yuh new environment. Yuh feel seh one day pass widout yuh a cross mi mine? No sah! Mi love fi mi big son only grow chronga wid each day weh pass by.

Me a fi yuh provida, an no matta how, me mek sure seh yuh clean, healty, ave food in a yuh tomach an shelta fi res yuh ead...So in answa tuh yuh question Son, no Agustus, me nuh ave no regrets.

Translation

I signed up for the Army back home, not in England. I volunteered in Jamaica and not long after completing the training I came to the UK. I had to leave you with Granny and stay rest assured that she would take care of you and bring you up in the correct manner my siblings and I were raised. She did that and more. I wanted to bring you-I would have carried you with me but I had nobody to take care of you whilst I was working. That was the only option which was viable at that time. Plenty of people immigrate, leave their families to go and work abroad all the time, do you think you are the first to get left behind? If you were in my position you would do the same wouldn't you? It's just how it is, because you can't make decent money in jamaica. Then when I got married and had the twins, I thought it would've been a good time to bring you over Agustus. I had plans to send you to school for the last few years of your school education, so you could have made something great for yourself. But then over time, Martin resented the thought of loving somebody else's child, that was the reason why we divorced. Then having to restart over again with the two children, it took a lot of time for me to get back onto my feet. I wasn't going to send for you to come over and bring you into chaos whilst you were settled back home. I had to make sure things were in order so you were able to flourish in your new environment. Do you think one day passed by without you having crossed my mind? No way! The love I have for my big son only grew stronger each day which passed by

I'm your provider and no matter how, I made sure you were clean, healthy, had food to eat and shelter to sleep under...So in answer to your question Son, no Agustus, I don't have any regrets.

Jeramiah, 22. Tall, stocky build, thick thighs, Bumper, clean shaven with a high top. He is sure of himself but not arrogant with it. He wears white chinos, a white fitted top and Blue Brogues, accessorised with a blue belt and a beaded necklace accompanied with a rope bracelet. It's spring. He's on a date with a girl he met at the gym earlier in the week. The restaurant's buzzing. They sit opposite each other on a table next to a window. Their eyes speak in flirtation and divert out of the window when it gets too much to bear. He previously asked her about herself, she's just returned the question. He really wants to impress her, he wants to show her he's serious about his passion but doesn't want to scare her off because of his dedication, so he's a little unsure how to play this. He really likes this lady, he wants her, and he is trying every tactic to keep her fully engaged and interested in him. He's not nervous on the surface but underneath he is trying to hide what he really feels.

Me a guh duh it. Me a guh buss di record, watch di ride. A long time me a work fi dis, since me a likkl yout an a watch Usain run a di trak, me know seh dis a weh me born fi duh. Me watch im time, an dat a weh me focus pan. Me nuh watch di res a di Atlete me a run wid, me wah beat di bes a di bes an nuh un les me a guh accep. Seven day a week me train, mornin an night, sun, rain, sleet, any kine a weda, it nuh mata, me outside a run. Sometime me use tuh guh dung an wach di bigga bwoy train.

Me spot im technique, ow im come outa di start block, attack di track, keep im shoula dong, relax, poised, focus pan di finish line yuh zimi? Sprinting is more dan a ten second run, a whole heap yuh a fi tink bout, a fi be mentally strong because di trianing ard. Yuh ave tuh be discipline in weh yuh duh, weh yuh eat when yuh sleep, di people yuh surroun yuhself wid, down tuh weh yuh wach an listen tuh. Me nuh guh out a night time too tough, fi tan up an feel mi ears a buss out. Yuh now ow much mile me coulda run in a di time me tan up an a dance? Back a day when me did a run fi di club an di man dem a pressure me fi guh a Danchall an ting, me use tuh dress like seh me a guh out, link up wid di man dem an guh missin alf way trough di night fi guh run-Mean time me a tell dem seh me link one Queen, but me nuh parr wid dem now b'cah like me seh likkl while ago, me focus pan di finish line...dis finish line.

Translation

I'm going to do it, I'm going to beat the record, watch and see. I've been working for this for a long time, since I was a little boy watching Usain run at the track, I know this is what I was born to do. I watch his time and focus on that, I don't watch the other Athletes I'm running against, I want to beat the best of the best and I'm not going to accept anything less. Seven days a week I train, morning and night, sun, rain, sleet, it doesn't matter what type of weather it is, I'm outside running. Sometimes I used to go down and watch the bigger boys train. I notice his technique, how he's come out of the start block, attacks the track, keeps his shoulders down, relaxed, poised, focused on the finish line, you get me. Sprinting's more than a 10 second run, there's lots you have to think about. You have to be mentally strong because the training's hard. You have to be disciplined in what you do, what you eat, when you sleep, the people you surround yourself with, down to what you watch and listen to. I don't go out at night much, to stand up and have my ears ringing-Do you know how many miles I could have run in the time i'm dancing around?

Back in the day when I was running for the club and the man dem were pressuring me to go out and stuff, I used to dress up like I was going out, link up wid di man dem and go missing half way through the night to go for a run- meanwhile, I tell them I've linked a Queen, but I don't hang out with them now because like I said a while ago, I'm focussed on the finish line.

This finish line.

Career Development Day

Spring 2033. At School. It is 11.27 am. Nadina is 16. She has a petite frame, brown skin and relaxed hair, which is back in a pony tale. She sees herself as a smart girl. She doesn't ooze confidence but she is sure of herself. She has a flair of womanhood about her because she is beyond her years. She's streetsmart and has great emotional understanding. She wears her School uniform. Black skirt, black knee length socks, white shirt, Blue jumper and tie. She's at her local comprehensive school which is situated in the middle of Birmingham. The group sit in a circle in the classroom along with their Teacher and a Nurse from the NHS. The group are sharing information about themselves and the reasons as to why they want a Career as a Medical Professional. The walls are covered in various educational displays. It's cold outside but it looks deceiving because it seems quite warm with the sun trying to peek itself through the clouds. One of her peers has just finished speaking, they've discussed his plans and applauded him. Nadina is about to speak but doesn't know what their response will be. She is nervous to speak, only because she is passionate and feels the pressures of making a career for herself. She's done a lot of research, so she knows what she is speaking about. Even though she's only been at the school for nearly three years, she is comfortable and confident with the School, Teachers and her peers.

She wants to make her Mother proud by choosing the right career path, but she needs to know if the choice she has made is the right one for her, not her Mother.

Suh, mi Mada sen me come a England fi guh live wid mi Aunty. Well a nuh mi Aunty by blood, she a mi Mada, Husban, Sista, Daughta. Anyhow, me come ere when me a tirteen an me a sixteen now, but when me lef Jamaica me tell myself as soon as me get di opportunity me ago kech flight back ome. But me deh ear fi nearly tree years now, an me like di frien dem weh me ave an di schooling weh me get, suh me nuh ready fi guh back ome yet.

pause

Oh, when me dun school me a guh work as a Nurse. Before, me did wah do Performin Arts, Acting, dat kina ting, cah me can Dance good, but mi Mada seh she neva sen me a forign fi guh prance up an dong pan stage. Mi Mada usban Sis/ Sonia, are name Sonia. She used tuh duh di Acting before she train fi be a Nurse. Basically di only reason she a Nurse now a trough di Covid nineteen pandemic, when all di Theatres close dem doors fi ow much mont, but di Government did a look fi volunteers an she did wah fi duh ar part fi elp out an support di Country, an a from dat she get in a di Nursin, an dat a di same reason why me wah be a Nurse-Not because me wah di Theatres fi close, because me wah elp di sick people dem, but di ongle ting me would a struggle wid a di blood because me dont like fi see it, but me try work roun dat.

(Takes cards out of her right pocket). Me did a look pan some a di course weh dem ave out deh, me mek a lis an call dem an ask bout di core subjects, assignments, placements...An di blood. (Puts cards back in her pocket) So...(Takes card out of her left pocket) Me mek anatha lis a di Medical Professions weh don't come in contac wid blood. Me call dem up, but when me mek di lars phone call, di Lady me did a talk tuh tell me dat dis might not be di bes profession fi guh in, because dere is every chance me will come across blood as a Nurse, an if me was tuh pass sombody a bleed out pan di street, by di Law me would a fi stop an give dem firs aid. Me ask are if me couldn' jus call one ambulance because if me a fi go elp out, a two ambulance dem a guh need...A trut she a talk Miss Nurse?...

Well, I don't tink dis a di right professional development group me in.
Mrs James, dem ave a Lanscape Gardenin development group? If me tell mi Mada me a study

fi be a Foliage Nurse, she would neva know di difference.

Translation

So my Mother sent me to England to live with my Auntie. Well, she's not my Auntie by Blood, she's my Mother's, Husband's Sister's, Daughter. Anyway, I came here when I was 13, and I'm 16 now, but when I left Jamaica I told myself as soon as I get the opportunity I'm going to catch a flight back home. But I've been here for nearly three years now and I like the friends which I've made and the schooling I get, so I'm not ready to go back home yet.

Beat

Oh! When I finish school I'm going to work as a nurse. Before I wanted to do Performing Arts, Acting, that kind of thing, because I can Dance really well, but my mother said she didn't send me to England to prance up and down on a stage. My Mother's Husband's Sis/ Sonia, her name's Sonia. She used to do Acting before she trained to be a Nurse. Basically the only reason she's a Nurse now is through the covid-19 pandemic, when all the Theaters closed their doors for how many months, but the government were looking for volunteers and she wanted to do her part to help out the country and it was from that she got into the nursing and that's the same reason why I want to be a Nurse-Not because I want the Theaters to close, because I want to help sick people, but the only thing I would struggle with is the blood because I don't like to see it, but I tried to work around that. (Takes cards out of her right pocket.) I was looking at some of the courses which they have out there, I made a list and called them and asked about the core subjects, assignment and placements...and the blood. (Puts cards back into her pocket.) So... (Takes cards out of her left pocket) I made another list of the medical professions which don't come into contact with blood. I called them up but when I made the last phone call, the lady I was talking to told me that this might not be the best profession to go in to because there's every chance I'll come across blood as a Nurse and if I was to pass somebody bleeding on the street, by law I would have to stop and give them first aid. I asked if I could just call an ambulance because if I have to help out they'll need two of them...Is what the lady said true Miss Nurse?...Well, I don't think this is the right professional development group I'm in. Miss James, do they have a landscape gardening Development Group? If I tell my mother I'm studying to be a foliage Nurse, she would never know the difference.

Wrong Road.

10.10am. Wednesday. 1991. Tall dark skinned woman in her mid 50s. She is a strong Black Female and head of the PRU. She wears a dress and cardigan with her Dreads and glasses. She's a professional Woman who doesn't look her age. A group of students have been sent to her office because of the rude behaviour they had been demonstrating to the cover Teacher. They sit as she speaks to them in her office, which looks very clean. It's a plain office barr posters of the school rules and regulations. It has a desk with computer equipment on top, a big filing cabinet to the right with two chairs opposite the desk. The group have been in the office for a while. She tries to reason with the students to show they are not alone, we've all done naughty things but we have to make a choice to change and grow out of it. We cut in part way through the conversation.

Me rememba one time back ome when me did a fiesty mi Mada. She tell me fi chry ar patient's one more time, si weh she a guh duh me, so me chry chucks it again wid ar but nuhun nuh appen...Till Friday afternoon. Me did juss dun school and ready fi guh ramp out a front wid mi frien dem. When me realise, Mummi pack up one bag an rest it pon mi bed. When mi guh pon di varanda an ask ar weh it fah, she git up, walk guh put on ar shoes, pick up di bag an dash it gih me. We kech bus an truck guh a Counchry. She nuh seh one word tuh me. We reach a di ouse-Me Mada Sister, Gloria. Wi sidung, drink one cup a Bush Tea an she guhweh lef me. Me bawl like me neva bawl before. Me wake up in a di night fi gah tailet, suh me outa back an all yuh ear a scuffle scuffle, me open up di door an when me shine di lamp in deh, a pure Cockroach me see, pan di wall, pan di floor...Mmm, back den, in a Country tailet a jus one whole dig out an one piece a bench mek up roun it wid zinc fi shelta. Me learn me lesson fi nuh feisty me Mada again. Suh why unuh nuh learn fi unuh lesson?

You teef firework from shop an guh fire dem after di police. You cut off one a di teacher hair. You mash out ow much window out a yuh last school an nuh stop trip people dung di stairs. You nearly blind one a yuh peers trough di sweeti you did a flick after ar an nuh stop beat people. You keep on a fill people shoes and tings wid glue and you don't stop try bun dung di place, and don't tell me nuh lie cah me see it pon video dis time Marcelle. Yuh know seh is one more strike fi unuh den next ting a courthouse an jailhouse. Me nah come look fi unuh! Me have di res a di School fi guide, if unuh nuh wah listen, den dat a fi unuh problem. We all get weself in a trouble, but di difference is some people learn from it an eders carry on b'cah dem wah di prison uniform an di clear bag when den dun serve dem time. Unuh wah dat accolade? Dat a weh unuh a aim fah, don't it?...Unuh nuh wah unuh owna business? Get big job, buy yuh house an cyar? Holiday home? Big savings account? Unuh really nuh want dat?...Di way some a unuh lie suh, would mek a good Prime minister. Stop lie, stop teef, stop di violence an show manners an respect. Mek sure unuh nuh end up in a mi office again. Tek dem a di isolation wing. Me soon come.

Translation

I remember a time back home when I was being cheeky to my Mother. She told me to try her patience once more and I'll see what will happen. So I tried it again with her but nothing happened...Till Friday afternoon. I had just finished school and was ready to play out with my friends. Then I realised Mom packed a bag and left it on my bed. When I went to the Veranda and asked her what it was for, she got up, went and put her shoes on, picked up the bag and threw it at me. We caught the bus and a truck to Country. She did not say a word to me. We got to the house-My Mother's Sister, Gloria. We sat down, drank a cup of Bush Tea and she went away and left me. I cried like I had never cried before. I woke up in the night to go to the toilet, so I'm out the back yard, and all you could hear is scuffle scuffle, I opened the door and when I shone the lamp in there, I saw nothing but Cockroaches, on the wall, on the floor...Mmm back then, most of the time the toilets in Country were just holes in the ground built with a bench around it and some zinc for shelter. I learnt my lesson not to be cheeky to my Mother again. So why haven't you all learnt your lessons? You stole fireworks from a shop and fired them after the Police. You cut one of the teacher's hair. You smashed so many windows out of your last school and kept tripping people down the stairs. You nearly made one of your peers blind because of the sweets you kept flicking at her and continue to beat people up. You keep filling people shoes and things with glue knowing that a particular person is allergic to it and you haven't stopped trying to burn the place down, and don't tell me it's a lie because I've seen the video this time Marcelle. Do you know It's one more strike for you all then the next thing is the courthouse and jailhouse. I'm not coming to look for youse! I have the rest of the School to guide, if you don't want to listen, then that's your problem. We all get ourselves in trouble, but the difference is some people learn from it and others carry on because they want the prison uniform and the clear bag when they've finished serving their time. Do you want that accolade? That's what you'se are aiming for isn't it? Don't you want your own business? Get great jobs, pay for your house and cars? Holiday homes? Big savings account? You really don't want that?...The way some of you lie, you would make a good Prime minister.

Stop lying, stop stealing, stop the violence and show manners and respect.

Make sure none of you don't end up in my office again. Take them to the isolation wing, I'll be there shortly.

Sasha, 23. Set in Jamaica. Saint Andrew. April, 1988. It's Friday, 37 degrees and it's late afternoon. She wears Green batty riders, Blue flip flops, a bright Yellow top, holy tights and a long red wig. Sasha has Just arrived home, carrying the carbolic soap in a paper bag. She has been desperate for the toilet since she was enroute back home but is full of excitement and has been fantasising about her future with Bakery Boy. She thinks he is the one for her and no other man can come close. She has just had a night and Morning full of passion and she is excited to tell her Sister about it. Sasha is all in with the situation she has found herself in, she has fallen and she has fallen hard. The way she speaks has a slight air of conceit but it is mere excitement that she hasn't had before. She thinks she knows what she wants. She and her Sister share the home their Mother onced lived in. The home is a small 2 bed cinder block house with a small Bathroom attached to the back of the house and a Veranda out the front. As you enter the Veranda, take a right into the living space, walk straight through where you will see the Kitchen. The walls are painted a pastel Blue colour. They have a warm feel to them and the objects in the home are old but we sense a timely feel to them, yet still clean and in good condition. Take a left where you'll find the Bathroom and left again is the door to the back yard. Sasha is going out to the back yard to piss in a bucket, as she does so, she speaks to her sister via the window above, delving into the antics of what happened when she left the house yesterday morning.

Danisha?...Danisha! Weh mek you deh in a di bartroom suh, ee? Night an day, day an night yuh in deh, always a fi a mek me a fi a pee pee round a back, wah pun tuh you, eh gyal? A man you ave in deh mek you tan suh?...(Goes to the bucket and starts to have a wee). When me lef yah yesideh fi di carbolic soap, a one piece a suttun dung a di alley, me suprise you nuh cum out di whole heap a commotion. Nuh Anitia a beat up Tumble out deh-Yuh know di syllable lick? Every time she talk, she lick him? She did a cuss him bout how im nuh sweep out di yard, but dis time im guh fi lick ar back, she suprise tuh backside. When di neighbour dem see dat, dem holla after are an dash water after ar. Mr Henry tek im in, seh im can stop wid im...Poor Tumble. Yuh remember di edda one weh run weh lef dem? Mi see im a town likkle while back, him look good. Mi gi im one 2 dolla an tell im fi hole on pon dat. Mi feel seh she a beat im b'cah is eida someting she learn as she a grow or she have problem wid herself.

Yuh a fi guh talk tuh ar dis time, tell ar she need fi talk tuh Tumble, an explain tuh ar how she a tek advance a di bwoy b'cah she might nuh even know she a tek advantage, fi all she know is how she suppose tuh raise dem...How she can a cuss im an she a sidun pon are behin whole day. Me can't talk tuh she b'cah any how she look pon me some type a way me cuss ar dung. You av di good patience, an she nah cuss me b'cah me up in are business. Teach ar fi communicate wid di bwoy before im turn pon ar. Is since Miss Julie dead she tun fool yuh know. Ey, listen dis! Mi fine a Man, me juss dun sex im likkle while ago. Im seh mi tight an di suhum sweet im yuh si. Im nuh all dat fi look pan but im sex good, an when im tell me seh im work a di bakery, me near drop dung. Me neva yet ave a boyfriend weh ave job...Im live wid im Mada an im two Sista, but dat soon a fi guh change b'cah me mek up one whole heap a noise, Bakery bwoy a fi guh fine one place fi wi live. Tear off likkle paper gih me, me nuh wah wet up mi draws. Im look like im get good money from im job b'cah im crep fresh an di amount a gold weh im ave on, im come in like Christmas decorations. (she takes the tissue from her sister which she has dangled from the window above)...But me wonda. Danisha, me wonda if im a guh propose tuh me...(pulls up her draws). You neva know, cah when dem fine a goodaz dem cyaa guh back- Me ave di brown kin an good air an mi toe dem pretty like penny, me nuh ave nuh Freddi Kruga foot like some gyal outa road, me look good/(A message comes through on her pager. She reads it, stares at it and looks disheartened from the information she has just read.) Me figet di Carbolic soap, me soon come. (She leaves abruptly)

Translation

Danisha?...Danisha! Why are you always in the bathroom? Night and day, day and night you're in there, making me always have to piss round the back, what's wrong with you girl. Is it a man you've got in there? (Goes to the bucket and starts to pee). When I left here yesterday to go to Town for the carbolic soap, there was such a commotion at the bottom of the alley, I'm surprised you didn't hear the commotion. Anetia was beating Tumble up out there-You know the syllable lick, everytime she talks she hits him. She was shouting at him because he didn't sweep out the yard, but this time he went to hit her back, she was so surprised. When the neighbours saw that, they shouted at her and threw water at her. Mr Henry took him in, he said he can stay with him...Poor Tumble. Do you remember the other one that ran away? I saw him in Town not long ago, he looks good. I gave him Two Dollars and told him to keep it. I think she's beating him because it's either something she learnt growing up or she's got problems. You're going to have to talk to her this time, tell her she needs to talk to Tumble and explain to her how she's taking advantage of her son, because she might not even know she's taking advantage, for all she knows that's how she's supposed to raise them...How can she shout at him and she sits on her behind all day. I can't talk to her because if she looks at me some type of way I'll shout at her. You've got good patience, and she's not shouting at me because I'm all up in her business. Teach her to communicate with the boy before he turns on her. Do you know it's since Miss Julie passed away she turned foolish.

Hey, listen to this! Ive found a Boyfriend and I've just finished having sex with him. He said my vagina is tight and it was so nice for him. He is not all that good looking but his sex game is good and when he told me that he worked at the Bakery I nearly fell down. I've never had a Boyfriend that has a job...He lives with his Mother and his two Sisters but that's going to have to change soon because I make a lot of noise, Bakery boys got to find a place for us to live. Rip off some toilet roll for me, I don't want to wet my knickers. He looks like he's on a nice wage because his trainers are fresh and the amount of gold he had on, he looked like he was a christmas decoration. (she takes the tissue from her sister which she has dangled from the window above)...But, I wonder. Danisha, I wonder if he's going to propose to me...you never know because when they find a good girl they cant go back-I have brown skin and nice hair and my toes are pretty like a pennies, I don't have Freddie Kruga feet like some of the girls out there, I look goo/ (A message comes through on her pager. She reads it, stares at it and looks disheartened by the information she has just read). I've forgotten the carbolic soap, I'll be back in a bit.

(She leaves abruptly)

Kevern's in his early 30s. He wears Jeans, Trainers and a Jumper. It's early 2000- He's at his local pub which is starting to get a little busy. There is a great buzz in the air, like something exciting is about to happen. There are glasses scattered on tables and the customers dotted around either wait to get served or chat away. The pub needs a revamp as the tired decor is still holding onto the 1980s. The walls are dreary and the furnishings worn. He has just bought another round of drinks and has asked the bar staff for the Dominoes. He brings the drinks over along with the Dominos and some peanuts and begins to play. This is the regular pub he and his friends attend on the weekend. He's familiar with the staff and the stale setting of the pub. They stock the drinks he likes and plays his style of music. Kevern suggests they play a game of dominoes so he can take his time to break into the conversation. He'ùs anxious about the men's reaction and is embarrassed about telling them the situation which occurred last night. As comical as it seems to them, he is serious in his speech. He explains as they continue the game. We cut in part way through the conversation.

Di uman mad! When we dun di game las night me go back ome...Arfta me visit mi fren, drink one bowl a soup an sekkle in front a di telivision. Bout one, two a clock me guh in a mi bed fi guh sleep. Me toss me tun, toss me tun whole night, den when me wake, me feel someting a watch me. When me open up one a mi eye, a nuh April a stan up ova me wid one jug. Me jump outa mi bed an ask ar a weh she a duh? An weh di backside she a du wid dat in a ar han? Yuh know weh di uman tell me? She tell me seh she ready fi pour hot oil in a mi ears-Me a fi ask ar if she sick in ar ead. She seh she ear pan road seh Kadeen a breed-Me tell ar she nuh fi listen tuh weh she ear a road- Double two!-B'cah sometime a nuh di full chrut. Me nu even one hundred percent dat Kadeen a breed fi me, so ow everybody pan street fi know?-Me a fi bawl out an tell ar seh me neva tell ar no lie weh day when me look ar dead in ar eye an tell ar “she a di only girl me a see right now”, me nuh lie, a she one me did a look pan. Next, she start fraat bout ow me lie tuh ar when me tell ar she one me did a dagga-Me a fi ask ar if sombady else did deh deh when we a sex, b'cah me only recall di two a wi did deh deh-Again, not one lie me tell ar, she shouda expan a likkle furda, dat a weh she should a duh. She love mek up noise yuh si.

Pause

But me learn mi lesson now, she nearly fry out mi brain an when me guh fi bead di nex morning, me realise she cut up di whole a mi garment dem. Me dun ramp wid uman now. She a good uman, me duh ar bad man...Suh ow me fi get ar back?

Translation

The Woman's mad. When we finished the game last night I went back home...After I visited a friend, drank some soup and settled down in front of the television. About one, two oclock I went to sleep. I was tossing and turning, tossing and turning all night, then I woke up sensing something was watching me. When I opened my eye, it was April standing over me with a jug. I jumped out the bed and asked her what she was doing here? And what the backside she was doing with that in her hand? Do you know what the woman told me? She said she was ready to pour hot oil in my ears-I had to ask her if she's sick in her head. She said she heard on the road that Kadeen's pregnant-I told her not to listen to what she hears on the street-Double two!-Because sometimes it's not the full truth. I'm not even a hundred percent sure that Kadeen's having my baby, so how does everybody on the street know?-I had to shout and tell her that I didn't lie to her the other day when I looked her dead in the eye and said she's the only girl I'm seeing right now, I wasn't lying, I was only looking at her. Next, she started arguing about how I lied to her about being the only one I was having sex with. I had to ask her if there was anybody else there when we were having sex because I only recall the two of us been there- Again, I did not tell her one lie, she should've expanded a little further, that's what she should have done. She loves an argument.

Pause

But I've learnt my lesson now, she nearly fried my brain and when I went to have a bath the following Morning, I realised she cut up all of my clothes. I've finished playing games with Women now. She's a good woman, I've done her bad...So how can I get her back?

Bloodclart.

It's 2015. Marcus is a tall dark skinned male, early 30's. He has a muscular build and shaved hair. He speaks with a very low basey tone. He's a hard working man and has just finished a twelve hour shift at a warehouse. He is very proud of himself and his Wife. However, he feels a little emasculated as they've been trying for a baby for a while now and they don't seem to be getting any closer. He wears jeans trainers and a white T-shirt. It's a Tuesday morning. The time is 8.07 am. He is in a supermarket which is in the opposite direction to where he lives. He stands in the aisle, not many people are shopping but a few staff are stacking shelves. The air is cold due to the air conditioning being on high. The items are neatly stacked and in order. Marcus is not unfamiliar to a Supermarket as he's an efficient man and a regular shopper, so he has a rough guide to the layout. The main reason for him being there is because he received a text message from his wife asking him to purchase something for her. He is unsure where to find the particular item and the specifics of what she requires. He's not shy about asking for help, he's calm and collected.

Uuuum...Nice. Pretty likkle ting, dat a weh me like. What a sight, beautiful piece a suhum. From di back from di front, any which way you look pon it, have di curves in a di right place. Look like it a guh fit nice, comfortable in a mi han. Di right size, nuh too big nieda too small, perfection a suhum you rarely see, but dis attractive sight weh me a lay mi eye pon, never in mi life me see suhum suh, suh/(phone rings). Alright Baby? Me deh a di supamarket, me jus a look pon suhum-Yuh want anyting in particular fi eat fi yuh dinna?...Me know yuh nah cook, me eva low yuh fi cook dem time a di mont? Weh yuh feel like baby?...Me jus pass di Ackee likkle while ago, mek me tun back an pick up one tin. Weh yuh want wid it, Spud an Cassava?...Well me nuh need fi get anyting fi di spinaz bcah we already ave flour an one bag a potato deh a yard suh is ongl di Cassava an Ackee me a fi get-Oh yes, mek me arsk somebady which part me can fine dem. Whole on, see one man ear, mek mi arsk im. "Excuse me Sir, do you so appen to know where I can fine a Lady item which prevents my wife from bleeding into her undergarments?...Whole on, me a fi guh a isle tree. Which one yuh want, di one weh you a fi insert or di one weh you a fi construc pan yuh panti?...Seen...Yuh have it strong b'cah di Man a talk bout di different level...(to the man) Weh you seh again?...(back to his wife!) Weh strength you want?...Alright baby me soon come-Him ask if you want some Femfresh fi guh wid it?...(pulls phone away from his ears)...Yuh want me fi pick up some chocolate fi yuh?...Whole on, Mada a call me

(cuts his wife off the phone)

Yes Mumi! You call at di right time. Yalright?...Me deh a di supamarket, a look me did a look pon some container...

Translation

Uuuum...Nice. Pretty little thing, that's what I like. What a sight, beautiful piece of something. From the back from the front, any way you look, has the curves in the right places. It Looks like it's going to fit nicely, comfortable in my hands. The right size, not too big nor too small, perfection is something rarely seen, but this attractive sight which I lay my eyes on, never in my life have I seen something so... so.../(phone rings). Alright Baby? I'm at the supermarket now, I'm just looking at something-Do you want anything in particular to eat for dinner?...I know you're not cooking, have I ever allowed you to cook at this time of the month? What do you feel like baby? I've just passed the Ackee a little while ago, I'll turn back and pick up a tin. What do you want with it, Spud and cassava?...Well, I don't need to get anything for the Spinners because we already have flour and a bag of potatoes at home, so it's only the cassava and AckeeI have to get-Oh yes, let me ask somebody where I can find them, hold on, there's a man here, let me ask him. Excuse Me Sir, do you so happen to know where I can find a lady item which prevents my wife from bleeding in her undergarments?...Hold on I have to go to aisle three. Which one do you want, the one which you have to insert or the one which you have to construct on your pants?...Okay...Do you have it strong because the Mans talking about different levels...(to the man) What did you say again?...(back to his wife) What strength do you want?...Alright baby, I'll be there soon-He is asking if you want some Femfresh to go with it?...(pulls phone away from his ears.) Do you want me to pick up some chocolates for you? Hold on Mother's calling me.

(cuts Wife off the phone)

Yes Mummy! You called at the right time. Are you alright? I'm at the supermarket, I was just looking at some containers.

To Be or Not To Be.

Tj (in his mid 20s) and his friends are at their friend's Barber shop. It's Saturday, 12:30 pm. He is dressed in the latest trend from head to toe. The other Barbers who work in the shop are familiar with Tj and his friends, they enjoy the energy they bring and the money too. There are 3 Barbour stations in the shop and two sofas for the customers. Tj tends to always take up one sofa, not because he's big but because he is loud and animated when he speaks, so his friends sit away from him when indoors as he tends to tap them when he speaks. The Barbour shop looks like a man cave, the only thing that has any sense of a female being in there is a shoe which has been by the coat stand for nearly a year...who knows who it belongs to or how it got there.

The day before, they briefly spoke about the issue they are now conversing about. It has been brought up again and they've been conversing about it since they entered the Barbours. They have all given their input and advice on the situation and now TJ is giving his closing speech (so to speak).

Yo, jus call di people dem an fine out weh dem a seh. Me see nuff man wait an wait, den when dem finally guh see wah gwan it too late. Me nuh know nuhun bout it till mi fada dead, an dem nuh teach we bout it a school...Me don't tink-Well, me cyar certify dat b'cah ongl likkle time me spen a school, an fi wi Mada an Fada nayn now nuhun bout it, suh ow we suppose tuh know? We a fi educate weself pan certain tings you know, some tings wi fi know an edda tings wi fi fine out weself. Yuh tan up yah fi ow long wid yuh phone in-Whole on, a di Blue Z4 dis? Nuh wonda you nuh wah call dem, anytime you start fi dial a two number yuh a press said time di way di phone likkle bit suh-Mek di blasted phone call an ear weh dem a fi seh!

Any a unuh get check before? Two time me see dem fi it an fimi prostate in a good shape. More time dem a guh book one appaintment fi you an tek blood from or du one scan fi see if anytin deh deh. Me duh all a dem, all a di tes, me tell dem fi mek sure. Me get MRI, dem tek blood from me, di uman alla stick ar finger in a mi batty fi mek sure nuhun nuh wrong-Weh you a look pan Me suh fa? If di uman need fi put ar finga in deh fi mek sure everything alright, me kin out mi Batty gih ar, no question, but she seh me nuh a fi du it suh, me jus a fi lay pan mi side, an yes, it urt, but me nah mek nuh finger stop me from mek sure everything alright. Me ave my fambily fi watch out fa. Between unuh, unuh ketch up in a fight ow much time and unuh fraid a finger? Tuh backside. Call di people dem an top waste me time.

Translation

Yo, just call the people and find out what they're saying. I've seen plenty of men wait and wait, then when they finally go and see what's happening it's too late. I didn't know anything about it till my father died and they didn't teach us about it at school...I don't think-Well, I can't be certain about that because I only spent a little time at school and our mother or father didn't know anything about it, so how are we supposed to know? We have to educate ourselves on certain things you know, some things we know and other things we have to find out for ourselves. You've stood there for how long now with your-Hold on, is that the Blue Z4? No wonder you don't want to call them, whenever you start to dial you press two numbers at the same time because the phone's are so small-Make the bloody phone call and listen to what they've got to say!

Have any of you got checked for it before? I've seen them twice now and my prostate is in good shape. They'll most likely book you an appointment and take blood from you or do a scan to see if anything there. I've done all of them, all of the tests, I told them to make sure. I had an MRI, they've taken blood, the woman even inserted her finger in there to make sure nothing's wrong-What are you looking at me like that for? If the woman needs to put her finger in there, I'll open my bum cheeks for her no question, but she said I didn't have to do that, I just had to lie on my side, and yes, it hurts, but i'm not making a finger stop me from making sure everythings okay. I've got my family to watch out for. Between you, you've been caught up in fights how many times and you're scared of a finger? Backside.

Call them and stop wasting my time.

Cum Arfa Bessitail.

Late 50s. England. Denville, male 43. He is clean, but rugged looking from his unshaven beard and unkempt hair. He walks slowly but still with a pace and observes everything he sees in deep thought. He is a lonely man just looking for company but cheery in his spirit. He wears clothing of his time-grey trousers, shoes, shirt, jumper and a coat. He carries a bag in his hand. The day is Bright, there is a light breeze in the air with a clear sky. The street is quiet but you can sense the hustle and bustle is about to emerge as parents begin their journeys to collect their children from the school over the road. There are houses on both sides of the street. He doesn't live there but comes here everyday to stand at the bus stop. He sees a mother and Child waiting for the bus to arrive. A man also stands a little further away, waiting for said bus. The child is in the pushchair playing with his toy cow. (The child drops the toy. Denville picks it up and hands it back to the Child). Denville begins to converse with the Mother of the Child.

Mi Granmada did ave one cow call Dessltail. She did Brown an of Jamaica hope breed. Granny put one bell pon she neck suh anytime a night it ring, she knows teef a try tek she weh. She did pretty yuh see. Ar eye dem did big an ar eyelash long, an when di sun shine it just glisten off a ar, mek she look like she av two colour. Nuh too long arfta me come a England, me get one call arfa Granny tell me seh she dead. She mussy did a wait fi me fi guh. Me did love ar yuh si...Every year she did breed a calf an true seh me did always in a chouble, Granny would save di calf fi bail me out. Me ketch up in situations with Man, omen, Man and omen, even Darg. Darg! Yuh can believe? Me nay wah fight, especially b'cah me did ave on mi white pants- Now, di darg come run me dung, come bite me pon mi leg and me a fi defend myself, so me shoo it weh. Now, di owner wah come fight me. Cut di long story shart, we near end up in a war, over Darg you know. Suh one time me did in a big chouble, nuh wid di Darg dis time-One next problem. Suh Granny sell tree a di cow fi get mi fare fi carry me a Englan. But di plane me come pan a nuh like dese plane yuh ave ere yuh know. It ave one wing come out suh, an anatha wing come out suh, but yuh did ave a string weh attach tuh di wing weh come in a di plane an yuh a fi hol on pon it, but when di plane get up, it guh suh...is a nice ride. Den yuh ave di wind...di turbulance, an di plane drop, yuh see it stop, yuh tink yuh belly a come out an when it stop, everybody start pray. Me did promise myself not tuh come on anatha plane again...Me come ere an live in one big ouse yuh know. 77 Arta Road. Yuh know ow much a wi did live deh? Forty two, in a di one ouse...Yuh ave one room, an yuh ave one bunk bed desso, anatha bunk bed desso, one desso, one drop bed an anatha drop bed ova yah, an we neva ave no eatin dem time you know, (laughs) an when you get off di bed yuh a fi step roun di people dem.

So we work ard an sen fi di res a wi fam/Oh yes, si it ere.

Translation

My Grandmother had a cow callled Bessitail. She was Brown and of Jamaica Hope breed. Granny put a bell on her neck, so if it rang in the night she would know a thief's trying to take her away. She was pretty, her eyes were big and her eyelashes long and when the Sun Shone, it glistened off her, made her look like she had two colors. Not too long after I came to England, I got a call from Granny telling me she died. She must have waited for me to go. I loved her so much. Every year she birthed a calf, truth being, because I was always in trouble, Granny would save the cow to bail me out. I've been caught up in situations with Men, Women, Men and Women, even Dogs. Dogs! Can you believe it? I didn't want to fight, especially because I was wearing white trousers-Now, the dog chased me and bit me on the back of the leg and I had to defend myself, so I had to shoo it away. Then, the owner wanted to come and fight me. Cut a long story short we nearly ended up in a war, over a Dog you know. So, once when I was in big trouble, not with the dog this time-Another problem. So Granny sold three of the cows to get the money to send me to England, but the Plane I flew on wasn't like the planes you have here you know. It had one wing which came out like this, and another wing that came out like this, but you had a string which was attached to the wing that came inside the plane and you had to hold onto it, but when the plane went up, it went like this, it was a nice ride. Then you have the wind...the turbulence, and the plane drops, you see it stop, you think your stomach is going to fall out and when it stops, everybody starts to pray. I promised myself I wouldn't fly on another plane again. I came here and lived in a big house you know. 77 Arthur Road. Do you know how many of us lived there? 42 of us, in the one house...In one of the rooms you had a bunk bed there, another one there, one there, a single bed and another single bed over here and we didn't have any heating in those times you know, (laughs) and when you get off the bed you have to step around people sleeping on the floor. So we worked hard and sent for the rest of our fam/Oh yes, here it is.

Tricky Situation

Derrick 40s. We are in the present, it's May. He sits in his kitchen, with his cup of cold tea beside his laptop. He wears his usual getup he would wear for work, suit barre his shoes. Just the fluffy socks. Mr Brown is teaching his lesson. He loves teaching his students. Prior to the lockdown, the class had started a project on flags and the history behind them. Katie has just given her feedback on the question Mr Brown has just asked. He can tell some are not engaged and sad to see many of his students unable to participate due to not having a device which supports that style of teaching. He cannot wait to get back into the school to continue the normal style of teaching. We open to see him speaking to his class via zoom as he's stuck teaching in this manner until this pandemic is over. He seems upbeat and excited to teach. After his session is complete we see his body language change and become anxious and nervous about a meeting he has to take part in.

The first section of the monologue is written in English but you can hear a slight Jamaican accent when she says certain words. You must take into consideration the Jamaican rhythm of the and intonations when articulating the text.

Thank you Katie, that was a beautiful description, well done. So let's just have a quick recap of the information we've learnt so far, making sure it is written down in your books and in your own interpretation please- I do not want it to be verbatim, marking 24 books with the exact wording is not exciting for me to read...So, suffering and hardship which had been encountered in the past along with the creativity and strength of it's people, Black. The fertile land which supplies great agricultural resources along with hope of the people, Green. Lastly the national wealth and beauty of the sunlight, Gold. Okay? Right, so moving swiftly on, for homework I would like you to create a flag which represents you, along with that I would like a written statement of what your flag symbolises. Any questions? Okay, Please submit it in the correct folder on your files. If you need anything at all, drop me an email Okay. Sign off please, see you all on Thursday.

(He shuts his laptop.)

Me cyar wait fi guh back a school, me feel fi di pikni dem bwoy. Tree a dem me nuh ear from, five nuh ave computa fi complete di work, an four a dem log on an me don't si dem. Dis situation messy, bwoy!...Mi belly bottom feel like it a guh drop out, me nervous man, yuh nuh nervous? Not even mi breakfast me eat dis mornin. Me did a look pan di paper dem again, fi see if me can gage weh kina a question dem a guh ask. Me nuh wah trip up an look fool I front a dem. Is eight a wi born and grow an me look after di whole a wi arfta mi Mada dead lef wi, suh me have experience a come outa mi ears. If everything guh tuh plan after we fill out di application form, six months time wi ave wi new addition. Me nuh know weh fi put on fi di meeting. Me walk pass one baby shop when me deya Town Tursday, it tek everytin inside a me nuh fi purchase di baby grow mi did a look pon. Lord strike me dung an brook mi neck if a lie me a tell, me tan up deh fi nearly fifteen minute a contemplate buy it...When we done sign di paper dem, we can guh a town pick up couple tings fi it?

Translation for end of text

(He shuts his laptop.)

I can't wait to go back to school, I feel for the children. Three of them I've not heard from, five don't have a computer to complete the work and four of them logged on but I haven't them. This situation's messy boy!...The bottom of my stomach feels like it's going to fall out, I'm nervous man, are you not nervous? I couldn't even eat my breakfast this morning. I was looking at the papers again, to see if I could gage the type of questions they're going to ask. I don't want to trip up and look stupid in front if them. Eight of us grew up together and I looked after us all after Mom died, so I've got experience coming out of my ears. If everything goes to plan after we fill out the application form, 6 months from now we'll have a new addition. I don't know what to wear for the meeting. I walked past a baby shop when I was in Town on Thursday. It took everything in me not to purchase the babygrow I was looking at. Lord strike me down and break my neck if I'm lying, I stood there for nearly fifteen minutes contemplating buying it...When we sign the papers, can we go into town and get a few things for it?

EhEh, She Lucky!

Present. Charlene is 32. She dresses well. Skirt, heels and a blouse. Her hair scraped back in a neat bun. Red lipstick and a little mascara. She knows her job and she does it to the letter.. It's evening. She stands in her high tech kitchen with her partner cooking. Pots are on the cooker boiling and ingredients on the side, some which have been used and others yet to be. They both like to cook together and have a nice solid relationship. She just wants to have dinner and a nice glass of wine but she has to get it off her chest, so she has her rant about her colleague, not giving way for any input from her partner.

Now, me nuh like fi seh it but me tell ar, me tell ar tree time but she nuh like listen, so me mek she carry on duh weh she did a duh. Jus because she ave hexecutive in ar title, she feel seh she entitle fi du weh she like an nuh a fi listen tuh constructive feedback, but when she ready fi criticise people she open up ar mout an nuh even draw fi breat till she dun talk. Now we en up wid fifty tousan, an all a dem ave defec pan dem. Ear ar wid ar excuse now " It must ave appen durin di production process " but even if it appen durin di process, you ave tuh keep yuh eye pan di produc every so oftin fi mek sure tingz like dat nuh appen, yuh undastan-So eida way Miss Entiklment fuck up, bout "Why did you throw me under the bus Charlene, we could have said it happend half way through", so she wah me fi lie fi ar an possibly lose fi me job fi she fi keep fi ar own-You mad! Darn faisty an out a arda "Because Ribeka, I told you about di default on di Machine tree time before you start pan di production, but you neva clean di wax out a yuh ears or else you would a ear weh me did a talk bout, dat a weh me shoud a seh tuh ar-Bout trow you unda di bus. But me see mi mistake now, instead a tell ar fi guh check pan it, me should a ask ar if she check pan it and explain further bout it when she neva check di firts time. Me believe she neva listen because a di way me tell ar fi check it, but sometime we Jamaican talk hard, an wi face look hard, we nuh realise di weight a weh we seh an ow we say it. Someting as simple as dat end up wid wi a quarril. All she did a fi do a listen tuh weh me a seh an explain ar feeling.

Usually we work good tugeda, since she come ere we never yet have cross words, but today, suhum mussy did wrong wid di two a wi mek wi nuh able fi understan di point di two a wi a try mek. Mi feel seh is one a dem day weh start bad an we cyar wait fi it dun.

Translation

Now, I don't like to say it but I told her, I told her three times but she doesn't like to listen, so I made her carry on doing what she was doing. Just because she has executive in her title she thinks she's entitled to do what she likes and doesn't have to listen to constructive feedback, but when she's ready to criticise people, she speaks and doesn't even take a breath until she's finished talking. Now we've ended up with Fifty Thousand and all of them have defects on them.

Listen to what her excuse was " It must've happened during the production process" but even if it happen during the process, you have to make sure to keep an eye on the product every so often to make sure things like that don't happen, do you understand-So either way Miss Entitlement has fucked up, asking" Why did you throw me under the bus Charlene, we could have said it happened half way through", so she wants me to lie for her and possibly lose my job so she can keep hers-Are you crazy! Damn cheeky and out of order "Because Rebecca, I told you about the defect on the Machine three times before you started on the production, but you didn't clean the wax out of your ears or else she would have heard what I was talking about", that's what I should have said to her-About throw you under the bus. But I see my mistake now, instead of telling her to go and check on them, I should have asked her if she had checked on them and explained further about it when she didn't check the first time. I believe that she didn't respond because of the way I told her to check it, but sometimes we Jamaicans talk hard, and sometimes our facial expressions seem unapproachable, we don't realise the weight of what we say and how we say it. Something as simple as that resulted in us arguing. All she had to do was listen to what I said and explain her feelings. Usually we work well together, since she came here we've never had an argument, but today, something must've been wrong with us both for us to be unable to understand each other's points. I think it was just one of those days which starts bad and you can't wait for it to end.

Pressure Point.

Tanisha 15. The year is 2016. Set in Santa Cruz, St Elizabeth. It's late afternoon. It has just been raining but still hot outside and her sister is drying the rain water from off the Veranda. The Veranda is painted pale orange, it has a concrete floor with a rug for decoration, four chairs and half a sofa propped up against the wall as if the sofa was made without a back. She wears house clothes, a simple dress and bare feet. She returned from school frustrated, annoyed and angry about the situation she and her friend found themselves in. She feels helpless and is looking for advice. Her Sister had noticed her frustration, so she had given her a pattie to eat as she knows food calms her down. As she sits on the Veranda she speaks about what happened and why she was fighting with her ex friend. Tanisha hates being told what to do, especially when she doesn't agree with it, which is what initially fuelled her vexation. Her sister asks her what happend to make her eat the Pattie in that way.

B'cah Sashein a chry tell me an Kadeen seh we a fi bruk wi virginity an top fi aid a hood. She seh we cyar parr wid dem from how we fridget suh, but a nuh suh it guh. Kadeen nuh like di bwoy a school b'cah some a dem too lie, dem bright an outa arda-An me nah sex Joozif cah a likkle time we a go out. Me value fi mi tuntun, dat a fi she bizniz if she nuh value fi ar own. Di intention fi im fi wife me mus deh deh, im nuh mek me im Queen yet suh weh me a free up mi sintin fa? Ear Sashein bout, if wi nah guh bruk it she nuh wah parr wid wi. Den she start talk bout ow suhum mussi wrong wid me b'cah me ave man an nuh bruk it yet. Me jus all ar up an tell ar ow mi kin nice, it nuh krack up an krani krani like fi she, me look good. My pumpum a nuh fi any an everybody, it nuh rubba out like fi she-She a close pin. When me an im ready, we du weh we wah du, she nah guh deh deh suh weh she a mek up noise fah? Me nah mash man fi keep on a parr wid people. Suh me tell ar is alright, me nuh walk wid people who chry pressure people fi duh certain tings. So me an Kadeen a guh start walk a school tuhgeda. Now she cyah stop taunt wi, she ala mek di res a di class tun gens wi.-But dat nuh badda mi, cah every mornin me walk outa gate armour up wid me elmit an breastplate, walk wid mi rod an staf, b'cah who God bless, no man curse. Kadeen nuh strong like wi, she a consida it fi mek dem stop taunt ar. Weh me fi duh bout Kadeen now?

Translation

Because Sashein's trying to tell Kadeen and I that we have to break our virginity and stop being scared of the dick. She said we can't hang around with them because she thinks we're frigid, but that's not true. Kadeen doesnt like the boys at school bcause they lie too much, they're cheeky and out of order-And im not having sex with Joseph because we havn't been going out long. I value my vagina, it's not my problem if she doesn't value hers, he has to have the intention for me to be his Wifey, he hasn't made me his queen yet so what am I giving it up for? Listen to what Sashein said 'if we're not going to break it then she doesn't want to hang out with us. Then she started talking about how something must be wrong with me because I have a man and haven't done it yet. I dragged her aside and told her how my skin is nice, it's not all cracked up like hers, I look good. My vagina is not for any and everybody, it's not rubbed out like hers-She's like a clothespin. When we're ready we'll do what we want to do, she's not going to be there so what's she making a fuss for? Im not having sex with guys just to keep hanging around with people. So I told her it's alright, I'm not going to walk with people who try and pressure people to do certain things. So Kadeen and I started to walk to school together. Now she can't stop taunting me, she even turned the rest of the class against us-But that doesn't bother me because every morning I walk out of the gate armoured up with my helmet and my breastplate, walk with my rod and my staff, because who God bless no man curse. Kadeen's not strong like us, she's considering doing it so they can stop taunting her. What am I supposed to do about Kadeen now?

Note- The clothes pin is a safety pin. It is a derogatory term related to females who freely give up sex. The mechanics of the metaphor is to squeeze the head of the pin and the legs of the pin will open.

Change Soon Come

2017.

Malcolm, Late 30s.

Wears Jeans, hoodie, trainers and a cap. He and his friends are at a meeting about a protest. One of his friends had recently died at the hands of the police. After being stopped in his car he was told to exit the vehicle without explanation. After stating that he was being targeted because of the colour of his skin, his car and his attire, the police proceeded to physically take the man out of his vehicle and began to restrain him. Due to the injustice the man faced, he fought for his rights and because he fought hard, the police couldn't match the force and tasered the man. Which was his cause of death. Today, friends, family members and other protesters are planning a peaceful protest to demonstrate the impact it has had on them. The grief weighs heavy on the community due to the inequality and the injustice from none of the officers being charged for his murder.

They're gathered at their local community centre where they are handing out banners and placards with slogans for the demonstration. Most people have a white T-shirt with a black DNA image drawn on.

We dehya...(clears throat) We dehya again. Dis is not a gadering me tek pleasure participatin in. How can one welcome people to such an event? We continue fi see dis pan a daily basis an we continue fi observe di lack a change. As we continue fi protes, we continue fi get shut dung. No more. No more! Dem a target wi yout. Target wi because a di colour a wi kin, by di texcha a wi air, by di clodes we put on, di lis dem go on an on. We see, we ear an we live di police brutality. People dyin at di hands of di Police. Dis a Murda, each an every time, an weh we receive from dat? Lie's an injustice's, rap up in dem scandalous apologies an deceitful cova up, time an time again. Dem cyar continue fi kill of wi people. Weh di justice? We still, tuh dis day observe di institutional racism widin society. Weh di equality deh? We fight fi dis everyday a wi life, nuh jus at meeting or when statement a mek ar protes a gwarn. Everyday when we step out a wi front door, we a fight!...Now, we all get inform bout di opposition weh seh dem a guh come protest gains wi, but we ago stan strong an stan firm. Police nah guh arres dem fi antagonize wi an taunt wi at wi owna protest-Di disorganise, animalistic, angry black people. We a guh duh it di right way. A peaceful, organised protest. We nuh deh deh fi fight-We deh deh fi get wi voice eard an start fi implement change. We, as a community, as a culture, as a race, we urt...an yes, dat mek wi angry, but we don't show dat in physical confrontation an criminal damage. No! We show it in a physical manifestation-We show it in numbers.

Me can guarantee if weh we ear right bout dem a come fi disrup wi protes, di police a guh chry fi prevent us from doin so, not prevent dem from attack us fi stanin fi wi rights. Dis a di time fi change. Ow much life a guh lars at di han a di police?

Di police who suppose tuh dedeh fi protec an serve, ow much before dem ear wi voice? We shouldn't be subjec tuh dis type a systemic discrimination. Not now not eva. Di time come. Dis is a new season. Dis should be no more. Dis will be no more.

Translation

We're here...(clears throat) We're here again. This is not a gathering that I take pleasure in participating in. How can one welcome people to such an event? We continue to see this on a daily basis and we continue to observe the lack of change. As we continue to protest, we continue to get shut down. No more. No more! They are targeting the youths. Targeting us because of the colour of our skin, by the texture of our hair, by the clothes we wear, the list goes on and on. We see, we hear and we live the police brutality. People dying at the hands of the police, this is murder, each and every time and what do we receive from that? Lies and Injustices, wrapped up in their scandalous apologies and deceitful cover-ups, time and time again. They can't continue to kill our people. Where's the Justice? We still to this day observe the institutional racism within Society. Where's the equality? We fight for this every day of our Lives, not just at meetings or when statements are being made or protests happening. Everyday, we step out of our front door, we're fighting...Now, we all got informed about the opposition who said they're going to come to protest against us, but we're going to stand strong and stand firm. The police aren't going to arrest them for antagonizing us and taunting us at our own protest-The disorganized, animalistic, angry black people. We're doing it the right way. A peaceful, organized protest. We're not there to fight, we are there to get our voice heard and begin to implement change. We, as a community, as a culture, as a race, we hurt...and yes, that makes us angry, but we don't show that in physical confrontation and criminal damage. No, we show it in physical manifestation-We show it in numbers. I can guarantee that if what we heard was right about them coming to disrupt our protest, the police are going to try and prevent us from doing so, not prevent them from attacking us for standing for our rights. This is the time for change. How many more lives are going to be lost at the hands of the police? The police who are supposed to be there to protect and serve, how many before they hear our voice? We shouldn't be subject to this type of systemic discrimination. Not now, not ever. The time has come. This is a new season. This should be no more. This will be no more.

We're in the present tense and it's a Saturday morning, around 10am. Outside, the sky is grey with a little drizzle. We're in an inner city high rise flat where Veronica and her flatmate live.
Veronica is a fluffy, light skinned woman, late 30s. She shows signs of bleaching from the darkness around her eyes, knuckles and cuticles. She's been bleaching her skin since she was a child. However, before she was able to bleach her own skin, her Mother had been using bleaching cream on her since she was 6 months old. She's always seen herself as not good enough because of the echoes of dark skin, hence one of her reasons for continuing to bleach in the first place.
Last night she had an epiphany. Today she has woken with a great air of confidence and commitment to changing. She's wearing pyjamas with her headscarf and spot cream dabbed on her face.

We see Veronica in her bedroom, the resemblance of a hair and beauty shop decorates her surroundings. She is currently putting all of her bleaching paraphernalia into a black bag. As she puts them in the bag she looks and speaks to her flatmate about the objects as though she is also reminiscing of the good and bad times of her bleaching days. This is unfamiliar territory for her. Her flatmate, also a Jamaican woman have a good relationship and run in the same circles. They briefly knew of each other back home through friends of friends but now find themselves living together. She is upbeat but we see an underlying nervousness which she tries to hide. She knows she has to do this and she knows it's going to be a difficult journey, no matter how blazè she seems about it.

Nuh more bleachin cream, me dun wid dat.

Goodbye tuh di Nadinola an di Dolly cream.

Me nah squeez nuh more jel in a di Idol lotion, nuh more rubbins fi me. Labamakozi, soun like kamikaze, dat a di inscription dem should a put pan di bottle. Karo white, Bio Claire, Abijan cream, me tun mi back, me serious me dun wid dat. Dung tuh di tights an long sleeve dem seh mek di bleach work betta, me nuh business bout dat, me dun bleach now, a my pocket a guh fatta. Brownin! Brownin! A dat me did wah fi ear. Is den yuh know seh yuh a turn dem ead, b'cah light skin is identified by Jamaicans tuh be fi dem quintessential. When yuh black in Jamaica, nuhbody nuh see yuh. Yoo blacki! A suh dem refur tuh you, but when yuh skin light, yuh feel seh di whole Parish a look pan yuh-Is den yuh feel good, an you don't a fi look far fi a bleachin cream. Guh cross di road a Miss wong. Dung a di street a pure vendor yuh a guh fine wid every bran a bleachin cream you can tink of. Me mek a conscious decision fi bleach, fi some Jamicans is a way of life. Yuh know seh di aspirations of black people wantin tuh lighten dem skin guh way back. Dis a suhum weh root deep widin di history of colonialism an indoctrination, weh pass down trough socialisation. When yuh skin brown in Jamaica, di more opportunity you ave. Plenty a time me guh a job intaview, as soon as di people dem see mi dem seh 'The role has been filled'. All now, in a disya time, light skin Jamaicans get see as higher class, even dough we come from di same place.

look! Kuh pan mi face, look ow it pachy pachy. It come in like Dalmation. See ow mi eye dem dark an dry from di chemical dem, come in like me get two box an don't even mek me start bout di whole heap a rash weh mi ave. We a fi mek a decision fi stop bleach up wi kin an teach wi pikny fi duh di same. We mus teach dem fi live comfortable in dem skin, b'cah right about now my skin a itch me tuh rahs.

Translation

No more bleaching cream-I'm finished with it. Goodbye to Nadinola and the Dolly cream. I'm not squeezing any more gel in the Idol lotion, no more rubbings for me. Labamskozi, sounds like kamikaze, that's the inscription they should have put on the bottle. Caro White, Bio Claire, Abijan cream, I've turned my back, I'm serious, I'm done with that. Down to the tights and long sleeves they say make the bleach work better, I don't care about that, I've finished bleaching now, my pocket is going to be fatter.

Browning! Browning! That's what I wanted to hear. That's when you know you're turning their heads, because light skin is identified by Jamaicans to be their quintessential. When you're black in Jamaica, nobody sees you. Yo Blackie! That's how they refer to you, but when your skin's light, you feel like the whole parish is looking at you-That's when you feel good. And you don't have to look far for bleaching creams. Go across the road to Miss Wong. Down the street you'll find nothing but vendors with every brand of bleaching cream you can think of. I made a conscious decision to bleach, for some Jamaicans it's a way of life. The aspirations of black people wanting to lighten their skin goes way back. This is something which is rooted deep within the history of colonialism and indoctrination, which is passed down through socialization. When your skin's brown in Jamaica, the more opportunities you have. There've been plenty of occasions I've gone to job interviews, as soon as they see me they say "the role has been filled". Even now in this time light-skinned Jamaicans get seen as higher class, even though we come from the same place.

Look! Look at my face. Look how its Patchi Patchi. It's like a Dalmatian. See how my eyes are dark and dry from the chemicals, It looks like I've got punched and don't even get me started about the rashes I have. We have to make a decision to stop bleaching our skin and teach our children to do the same. We must teach them to live comfortable in their skin because right about now my skin is itching me.

Slave. (Name unknown) She's in good health, small but has an athletic frame. Her hair is cainrowed in two plaits, as petite as she is for her age, she's Talawa. She wears a long dress with her apron over the top and bare feet. It is 1693 Saturday 12th of November 10.43am. Slave was literally born enroute to the plantation on board ship "Return". Her Mother passed away during childbirth, leaving slave in the care of the next person who had laid beside her Mother since boarding the ship. Slave has been at the plantation ever since her arrival, she has seen nothing else but the other Slaves that have come, gone and returned. She doesn't tend to keep friends on the plantation except Chunk and Grumble. Chunk's like a Mother to Slave, she's taught her everything she knows. She's the only person she trusts with her life. As a whole she trusts the group to get her to freedom but other than that, just Chunk and Grumble. Slave doesn't want other slaves to come to the plantation as they might be informers and all the work they have done to get this far in order to get closer to freedom, would be for nothing. Trust is a very important part of Slaves life, we don't know specifically why but she has issues surrounding that. Slave had been upstairs in Masters bedroom. The fixtures are of Georgian style with Mango wood floors, tray-like ceilings and a large four poster bed taking up the majority of the space. Everything has its place in the room and is decorated immaculately. Slave was making up the bed, as she was doing so she heard voices from beneath her coming from the counting house. She listened out for information from Mater and the Gentleman he was speaking to, as the information may be of some importance to the slaves in order to gain their freedom. Whilst she eavesdropped she still continued to make noise in order not to give herself away. She isn't nervous about it, she's done it plenty of times and not gotten caught yet. She holds her breath when she puts her ear to the floor and gets up for air when needed. She's currently in the kitchen cleaning the floor whilst Grumble makes tea, as they do so, Slave informs her of the conversation she overheard.

Hey! Yuh recall a while ago when Chunk tell wi new slaves a come? Well, a trut she a talk. Dis mornin when me a mek up di bed in a Masa room, me ear im an Man a talk dungstairs, suh me kiss mi ears gens di groun. Me ear dem a talk bout one Negro sale at di Tavern tomorrow. So, Masa ask Man if im pick dem out, im seh im pick im out di bes slave from before dem come ashore an im a guh keep dem pan board till sale dun. So eida way new slave a come a di plantation...Me nuh like new Slave, dem look pan me like mi different, dem tink me a Masa Daughta an call me Mongrel when we a quarril, but a Arawak me be an proud a it- Me ope dem big like bull so Masa sen dem a fiel fi guh wuk, den we nuh a fi chat tuh nobody. But like ow di revolution close, di slave could ala get win a it an inform pan wi, den we neva able fi get free. Is Chunk mek me know ow long wi ave till we get wi freedom, an she know b'cah she always a fi a fan dat dyam likkl Hedward when im deh a school. She see pon im paper yesideh- Friday, November, Twelve. Dat mean Freedom day soon come, but all she, she a fi guh mine weh she a duh b'cah anyhow Masa fine out a learn she a learn, a big punishment she a guh get. Chunk seh when we get it, tings nah guh be di same again. Jus like when Horice dead...Likkl while afta im come a di plantation, Masa seh im an Chunk a fi wed-Im ongl wah Marry wi of fi get more slave, but Horice dead a while ago now, an Chunk lef wid di two pikni, Adove an Tar-A Marsa name im suh b'cah im born Black like tar but im lighten up now suh im name nuh match weh yuh see.

Pause

Me nuh know if me wah mi freedom. Weh me suppose tuh duh when me get it, weh me fi go?

Shorter pause

If me get kech, all dem a fi do a draw di clodes arfa mi back fi see which part me come from, an carry me come right back ear. Me see nuff runweh get kech an bring back an see Masa du whole eap a evil tings. Yuh see sometime when me a lay a night time, me tink bout some a di slave weh run weh an nuh come back, if dem dead or alive...Weh fidem freedom feel like?...Weh it a guh feel like fi we?

Translation

Hey! Do you recall a while ago, when Chuck told us new slaves were coming? Well, she was talking the truth. This Morning when I was making up the bed in Masters room, I heard him and Man talking downstairs, so I put my ear to the floor. I heard them talking about a Negro sale at the Tavern tomorrow. So, Master asked Man if he picked them out, he said he picked him out the best Slaves before they came ashore and he's going to keep them on board until the sale is over. So either way we're going to have new Slaves come to the plantation. I don't like new Slaves, they look at me like I'm different, they think I'm Master's Daughter and call me a Mongrel when we argue, but I'm Arawak and I'm proud of it-I hope they're big like Bulls so Master sends them to work in the field, then I won't have to speak to them, but considering the revolution is close, the Slaves could hear about it and inform on us, then we'll never get free. It's Chunk who lets me know how many days we have till we get our freedom and she knows because she always has to fan little Edward when he's at School. Yesterday, she saw on his paper-Friday, November 12. That means freedom's nearly here, but she has to be careful what she's doing because if the Master finds out she's learning she'll get a big punishment...I don't even know what that means. Chunk said when we get it, things aren't going to be the same again. Just like when Horice died...Not long after he came to the plantation, Master said he and Chunk had to get Married-He only wants to marry us off to have more Slaves, but Horice died a while ago now and Chunks left with two children, Adove and Tarr. It was Master who named him that because he was born Black like tar but he's lightened up now so his name doesn't match what you see.

Pause

I don't know if I want my Freedom. What am I supposed to do when I get it , where am I supposed to go?

Shorter pause

If I get caught, all they have to do is rip the clothes off my back to see where I'm from, and carry me back right here. I've seen many runaways get caught and bought back and seen Master do loads of evil things. You know, sometimes when I lay awake at night , I think about some of the Slaves who have run away and not come back, if they're dead or alive...What does their freedom feel like?...What's it going to feel like for us?

1941.

Spring, 1974. Abigail's at a hospital. She had travelled alone and is now speaking to a member of staff. Due to her slight erratic behaviour and confusing conversation when she entered the maternity ward, one of the Nurse's had shown Abigail into a side room in order for her to privately explain her reasons for being there. She sits on the edge of the bed as they continue their conversation. She wears a dress, black shoes and a long coat. The hospital is busy, you can hear the muffled echo from the hustle and bustle outside the room. The room itself is painted mint green with drawings of cartoon characters, which seems like it has been painted by an inebriated Artist. It has a bed, chair, bedside cabinet, sink and a plastic plant which may have been left by a previous patient or the hospital. Even though the room is bright and colorful, we get the feeling of a cold, clinical and regimented ora which Abigail was once accustomed to. This is one of the many Hospitals which Abigail had added to her list to contact regarding her issue. Abigail expected to be turned away as she had been on several other occasions but because her approach was different, this Nurse saw a deep hurt in her, she took pity and offered her a space to speak. Abigail has never been this far in terms of speaking to someone about it. She is a little taken aback and somewhat reserved as she now doesn't know what to say. Even though she's of age, her speech and her body language has reverted back to the childlike manner she had at the time of the incident, giving clarity of the weight of the trauma she suffered after having her baby taken away from her. We cut in part way through their conversation.

Im a flourish. Im get feed, water, care everyday...Im a get big now. Im colour a get more intense, im a get darka an darka by di day. Yesideh, me a prune im an realise one a di new leaf a open up. Me stroke it an tuck mi finga underneat. It curl right roun it, same said way like mi precious. A suh me did call ar, Precious...Decemba Twelve nineteen farty one...

(smiles)

Di wuss day a mi life. Tree farty seven inna di mawnin, mi Precious baan. Me manage fi ketch two glimps a ar an by Tree Fifty Two, me nuh see ar again. Ar likkle round face, big nose, brown skin...She smell...Ar smell...Ar skin smell like...Nuttun yuh ever smell before. Me did mek one crochet one hat fi ar but she neva even able fi even try it on. Me know seh it would a look nice pon ar, me juss know...it did pink wid one likkle yellow bobble pon it.

Beat

Me tell Mama fi guh see wah pun tu ar, but she jus sidung deh, 'jus tink bout yuh heducation, yuh is good at yuh school work'- Eva since da day me wonda wah pun tuh ar. Me nuh sleep a naytime at all at all... Arfa me come out a arspital an reach back ome, me get nuhun but chroubl. Dem a bawl out sketell when me a walk pon road, fling rock arfa me, ask me if me dash di baby a riva- whole heap a fuckri...Everybody know me did a breed, but chrue seh Mama did shame. Yuh know ow much time me ask mi Mada wah pun tuh mi baby? She jus tun ar face from me each time me ask-Di lars time me ask ar, me scream in ar face when she did a sleep. She kech ar fright. She guh fi pull di sheet an tun ova fi guh sleep again. Me draw di sheet arfa ar, an when she get up fi get di broom fi lick me dung, me run out a di ouse. Me nuh si ar again. All no, me still nuh know wah pun tu mi baby, an dat a why me dehya, me wah fi know weh she deh.

Beat

You can help me fine out wah pun tuh ar?

Translation

He's flourishing. He gets fed, watered, cared for every day...he's getting big now. His colours getting more intense, he's getting darker and darker by the day. Yesterday I was pruning him and realized one of the new leaves opened up. I stroked it and tucked my finger underneath. It curled right around it the same way my Precious did...That's what I called her, Precious...December 12th 1941...(smiles) The worst day of my life. Three Forty Seven in the morning my Precious was born. I managed to get a glimpse of her, and by Three Fifty Two I didn't see her again. Her little round face, big nose, brown skin. She smelt...Her smell...Her skin smelt like... Nothing you'd ever smelt before. I made a crocheted hat for her but she didn't even get to try it on. I know it would've looked nice on her, I just know. It was pink with a little yellow bobble on it.

Beat

I told Mama to go and see what happened to her but she just sat there, "Just think about your education, you're good at your school work". Ever since that day I've wondered what happened to her. I don't sleep at night at all... After I came out of Hospital and got back home, I got nothing but trouble. They shouted out skettel when I walked on the road, they threw stones after me, asked me if I threw my baby in the river-loads of terrible things...Everybody knew I was pregnant but because mama was shamed. Do you know how many times I asked Mama what happened to my baby? She just turned her face from me each time I asked-The last time I asked her, I screamed in her face when she was asleep. She caught a fright. She went to pull the sheet back up and turn over to go back to sleep, I pulled the sheet off her and when she got up to get the broom to beat me, I ran out the house. I haven't seen her since. Even now to this day, I still don't know what happened to my baby, and that is why I'm here, I want to know where she is.

Beat

Can you help me find out what happened to her?

Home From Home

Brittany. A Jamaican National. Mid 20s. September 2nd, 1996. 10am. She sits in a room speaking with a Lawyer. The room is warm and quite modern for its time. The Holding centre is surrounded by nothing but fields. She wears leggings, a top and pullover jumper with slip on shoes. With her being caught by the immigration she sees herself as a failure. She's annoyed with herself but she knew she had no choice to do what she did. Everybody knows Brittany in her Parish and if they don't know her, they know of her. The Minister's Homosexual Daughter. Since the revelation of her sexuality she has been running from her community, then ran from her country to settle in England where she now resides with her partner. Brittany has been working on her application for her indefinite stay, but has been working illegally to earn money to support herself whilst her application is being processed. The morning before this monologue, Brittany went to work where she cleans at a party venue. The immagration stormed the building and Brittany and others were taken to the police station, then later to a Holding cell where they will be deported back to their National Countries. This is Brittany's first time in a situation like this. She's not in fear as she is aware of what to expect but in her heart she's extremely sad at the prospect of it. All Brittany wants to do is live an honest, simple life, but now she has less chance of seeing that happen. She sits, listens and explains, all in a calm manner.

I would neva step foot back pan dat soil again. Me rada...Me cyar guh back ome an live di same way me did a live fi di pas five years ova ere. Yuh know weh it tek me fi reach yah?
When my Mada an Fada fine out seh me a homosexual, im tek di machet lick me dung. If a nuh fi mi Mada, a kill im would a kill me out deh. Den when di Parishna dem fine out, di Pastor seh mi Mada an Fada a fi guh a di Christian counselin.

Dem did seh dem wah fi chry mek out if is dem weh mek me gay from di way dem bring me up-But if dat a di case mi breda an sista wouda gay, nuh chrue? All troughout dat time dem seh me mentally unwell.

Dem fool me seh we did a guh out, carry me a one man. Me nuh know weh im duh but me vomit out green like a bag juice me did a drink. Yuh know ow much time me get rock fling arfta me?
One time, one bag a man set pan me, seh dem a guh convert me cah me nuh suppose tuh lie wid next uman-Me neva run suh fas in a mi life, an dat a di firs time me did a fi lef mi Parish guh stay a Counchry. Me cyar guh true dem kina tings again. Me sekkle down ova ere now, me have mi place weh me fix up nice an di likkle fren weh mi have. Mi Girlfrien a guh mad-Even dat, weh me a guh duh bout she? Yuh feel seh she a guh come ova come stay? After weh me tell ar, yuh mad?
Everyting jus mash up now...Everything did start fi work out, now me dehya cage up like Darg. All me

did wah do a sekkle an live good. All now my Mada an Fada a pray fi cure mi illness, an uh nuh still wah sen me back?

Translation

I would never walk on that land again. I would rather...I can't go back home and live the same way I've been living for the past five years over here. Do you know what it's taken for me to get here?
When my Mother and Father found out I was a Homosexual, he took the machette and wouldn't stop beating me with it. If it wasn't for my mother stepping in he would have killed me out there. Then when the parishioners found out, the Pastor said my parents had to go to Christian Counselling. They said they wanted to try and work out if it was them who made me gay from the way they'd bought me up-But if that was the case then my Brother and Sister would be gay too, wouldn't they?
All throughout that time they were saying I was mentally unwell.

They fooled me saying we were going out, they carried me to a Man. I don't know what he did but I vomited Green like I had been drinking a tip-top. Do you know how many times I got stones thrown at me?
Once, a group of men chased after me, they said they were going to convert me because I wasn't supposed to sleep with Women. I've never run so fast in all my life, and that was the first time I had to leave my parish and go and stay in the countryside. I can't go through all of those things again. I've settled down over here now, I've got my place which I've decorated nicely and the few friends which I've made. My girlfriend's gonna be mad-Even that, what am I going to do about her? Do you really think she's going to come over and stay? After what I've told her, are you mad? Everythings just falling apart now... Everything was starting to work out, now I'm here caged up like a dog. All I wanted to do was settle down and live good-Even now, my Mother and Father are praying

to cure my illness and you still want to send me back?

Watch Di Pale

Nanna stands there in her bed clothes, head scarf and slippers. It's a calm breeze outside and a few people are walking on the road. It's Sunday, 1976. The children always sleep at nanas on Saturday. She still isn't used to having all six, even though it's a regular occurance. The Door knocks and she answers it...It's the bread and pops man. They know each other well as he is a good friend of the family. He delivers her shopping and they begin to have a natter. Bread man always delivers on Sunday, because the bread is always fresh. This is a convenient service for her and others of the time. She wants to get back to the kitchen because Markus is in there...alone. He likes biscuits and he knows exactly where they are.

Me nuh know bout a good Mornin, di whole a di pikini dem a drive me crazy but im alright, yuh know ow im stay aready. Yuh come jus in time. Tanks, yuh ear. (the man at the door doesn't move, he is staring at Nanas attire and the bandage she has on her wrist)...A mi han yuh a look pon? Nuh Marcus. Me git up dis Mornin an a walk dungstaire, who tel Markus fi come follow back a me, two twos im kech underneat mi foot, di two a wi tumble ova, mek me a fi dash di pale fi kech miself an im sed time. Me scare fi mi life an im a look up in a mi mornin a laugh. Den im start bawl bout im wah breakfars. Arfta me mek di food fi di six a dem eat, im seh im dont want to eat dat. (Goes to hand her another bag) No, is alrait, me ave food in a di cupboard, but tanks fi offa-Suh, me lef im an di ada one fi guh baid di res a di pikin dem, when me cum back in a di front room, im near eat of one packet a digestive an a jump up an dong pan di setee. Me tell im no, eheh! Me a fi ask im weh im tink im a duh. Mi bade im ready fi put on im cloads, ear weh di bwoy tell me "I dont want to wear that, I want my blue top"-A big man me ave in deh yuh know. Anyway, tanks fi di bread...Me a guh mek one cup a

Tea an cut one slice a hard dough bread an eat wid likke condense milk now (he doesn't attempt to move)...If mi ouse did in a arda an nuh suh full, me tell yuh fi come taste di bread (still doesn't move)...If yuh debout tomorrow pass by, me mek up one sandwich fi yuh lunch, aright? Good night.

(He smiles and walks away, she turns to go back inside)

Oh Lord!...Markus? yuh deh?

Translation

I don't know about a good morning. All of the children are driving me crazy but he's all right, you know what he's like. You've come just in time. Thanks, okay? (The man at the door doesn't move, he is staring at Nanas attire and the bandage she has on her wrist)...Is it my wrist you're looking at? I got up this morning, walking downstairs, who told

Markus to come and follow behind me, next thing I know he's caught up underneath my feet and the both of us tumbled over, making me have to throw the pale to catch myself and him at the same time. I was scared for my life, he was looking up in my face and laughing. Then he started crying about wanting breakfast. After I made the food for the 6 of them to eat, he says he doesn't want to eat that (Goes to hand her a bag)- No, it's all right, I've got food in the cupboard, but thanks for the offer-I left him and the other one to go and bathe the rest of the children. When I came back in the front room, he nearly ate a whole packet of digestives and was jumping up and down on the sofa. I told him no! I had to ask him what he thought he was doing. I gave him a bath ready to put his clothes on, listen to what the boy told me." I don't want to wear that I want my blue top"-I've got a big man in there you know! Anyway, thanks for the bread...I'm going to make a cup of tea and cut a slice of hardo bread and eat with a little bit of condensed milk now...(he doesn't attempt to move) If my house wasn't so full,

I would've invited you In to taste the bread (still doesn't move). If you're around tomorrow, pass by, I'll make up a sandwich for your lunch. Okay? Good morning. (He smiles and walks away)

Turns to go back inside.

Oh Lord...Markus?

Where are you?

Multipurpose.

Spring, 2017. It's Tuesday Morning and Zendell, 55 is visiting her sister at Bellevue. She wears a blue frock and flip flops. Her hair is plaited in four doo doo plaits. This is the first time she has visited her sister since she arrived. Zendell had spent the morning cleaning up Popas plot, which is on the same land as the house. The house is somewhat unkept and in disarray since her sisters sudden decline and admittance to Bellevue. Unfortunately, Zendell's Sister is the only one in the family left living in Jamaica. After the death of their Father, her neighbour Deloris is the closest thing she has to family over there. Zendell had bought a bag of clean clothes and a little bag of sentimental items with her to the hospital...Her crochet blanket, plastic flowers, a doyley to rest the vase on, and a few photos and ornaments. Whilst visiting her sister she unpacks her clean clothes and packs her dirty clothes in the bag, ready to take away with her. Her sister is asleep, or so she thinks. She takes the newspaper out of her bag, sits beside her Sister and begins to read to her. Eventually, frustrated with the heat, Zendell gives up on reading the newspaper, folds it in half and begins to fan herself with it. She diverts her attention to her sister. Throughout this monologue, Zendell goes between fanning herself and her Sister.

Wah pun pretty lady? Me did a clean up Popa dis mornin-See ow yuh eye dem a flicker, if nuttun else me know seh yuh recall Popa...Me carry fresh clothes put in a di sintin, and when me lef ya me a guh carry back di dutty clothes fi guh wash, but me cyar come tomorrow cah me a fi guh a town fi sort out di paper dem fi di lan...You know seh it did too much fi you one hangl, me nuh know why you nuh talk seh is help you did need...Everything overgrow bad. A di cutlass me did a fi draw fah fi fine Daddy yuh know. Dung to di tree dem weh bare fruit, dem drop arf an rotten, pure Mongoose come nest in deh...a dat blarsted Bancroft weh carry dem come mek di place tun suh. Dyam bullfrog!(kisses teeth)

Me chry polish di plaque likkle but chu seh di weather wear it out, di side dem start crumble weh when me a wash it dung, but me give it one lick a paint and go ova di likkle writing weh fade weh, suh it nuh look too shabby. Mi nuh know how long it a guh stay suh. Me give Deloris likkle change fi wash im dung once a mont fi di year, an fi mek sure im plot nuh overgrow...Me did a clean out di house an me fine im knife, yuh recall?...Im use it fi pick stone outa im shoes, tek off di dead skin from im eal back, cut up bulla cake-All kine a tingz. It come in like im did deya war wid im survival kit, but Granny did ave whole heap a equipment fi clean, cut, slice, polish, everytin! Suh me nuh know weh im did a gwarn wid. Popa knife universal, anytin guh!

Beat

Me remember one time afta me come ome from school, im ask mi if mi want Mango, me seh "yes please", im cut di Mango give me, an me tek it an start nyam it, but me notice one black sintin pan it, suh me flick it off an carry on a eat it but when me dun nyam it, me see im tek out one knife an start fi clean out di groove a di cabinet. Me tan up de a look pan im, realise a di sed knife im use fi cut up mi Mango, me spit like me neva spit before. Me use tuh love Mango when me a pikni, but when me see dat, me nuh eat it again, neida Bulla cake

Beat

Deloris talk seh one man cyar dun pree pon di lan, an she tell me seh yuh tell him fi guh bout im business, suh me nah sell it gih dem...Bwoy sah, me nuh know weh me fi do. Me cyar manage look arfta it from back home, and Deloris cyar keep fi are eye pon it fi more dan a year or suh, cah she soon dead. Weh mi fi do wid di land now, ee Sis?

Translation

You alright pretty Lady? I was cleaning up Poppa this morning-Look how your eyes flickered, if nothing else I know you remember Poppa...I brought fresh clothes and put them in the thing, and when I leave I'm going to carry back your dirty clothes to get washed, but I can't come tomorrow because I have to go to Town to sort the papers out for the land. You knew it was too much for you to handle, I don't know why you didn't speak up and say you needed help...Everything's overgrown real bad. It was the cutlass I had to use to find Daddy you know. Even the trees which bear fruit are falling off and rotting, loads of Mongoose have come and nested in there...It was that bloody Bancroft who brought them here and made the place turn out like this. Dyam bullfrog!(kisses teeth). I tried to polish the plaque a little bit but because the weathers wore it out, the side started to crumble away when I washed it down, but I gave it a lick of paint and went over the writing that had faded away, so it doesn't look too shabby. I don't know how long it's going to stay like that. I gave Deloris some change to wash him down once a month for the year and to make sure the plot doesn't overgrow...I was cleaning out the house and I found his knife, do you remember?...He used it to pick stones out of his shoes, take the dead skin off his heel back, cut Bulla cake-All sorts of things. It was like he was at War and it was his survival kit, but Granny had all kinds of equipment to clean, cut, slice, polish, everything! So I don't know what he was doing. But Papa's knife is universal, anything goes!

Beat

I remember this one time after I came home from school, he asked me if I wanted a Mango, I said "yes, please," he cut the Mango, gave it to me and I started to eat it, but I saw something black on it, so I just flicked it off and continued to eat it but when I finished eating it, he took out the same knife and started to clean the groove in the cabinet. I stood there and looked at him, realized it was the same knife he cut my Mango with. I spat like I've never spat before. I used to love Mangos when I was a child, but when I saw that I couldn't eat it again that nor bulla cake.

Beat

Deloris said a man won't stop coming to look at the land, and she told me you told him to go about his business, so I'm not going to sell it to him...Oh boy, I don't know what to do. I can't manage the land from back home, and Deloris can't keep her eye on it for more than a year or so because she'll be dying soon. What am I supposed to do with the land now, eh Sis?

Fish Friday

Morning. The year 2004.
At a food shop in South London.
Peter, plumpish Male, in his early 50s
He and his colleague are in the kitchen of the Food shop prepping food for the day's shift. They also have to scale, gut, season and cook a large amount of Fish, as they cater for a Dance which is kept on the last Friday of every month. The kitchen is small, dark and dingy. It has a little island in the centre for prepping with the essential domestic appliances around the edges of the kitchen. The back door is propped open which brings the much needed daylight into the space. Peter wears tracksuit bottoms, trainers, Tshirt, an apron, gloves and a hair net. Playing in the background is a local pirate radio station, the song by Capelton, That day will come plays but gets wheeled up. He speaks with his colleague about what had happened the night before.

Yuh nuh see how me reach a work tideh? One piece a passa passa yesiday evenin, me nuh know wah pun to Tamisha, she tek set pon me bout di food weh me a eat an ow me nuh exercise an all dem ting. A di Jelly me did a eat, me a fi ask ar which one a wi a di adult roun ya. She come in like she push me out. She did a talk bout she nuh wah me dead suh me a fi get exercise an start fi eat good. She come in like ar Moda, always a fuss bout somting ar aneda. She box it out mi han! Me a fi cuss ar an tell ar nuh fi treat people suh, an low me wid mi jelly...Me ave mi bicycle out a back-Yo Jerki! Jerki! look weh me fine in a di Fish. Look! Mi see suhum in a di mout, when me start fi gut it me realise weh it be. No man! Dis nuh right.
Soon we cyar eat a good food because wi mash up di blarsted ocean-Too lazy fi clean up afta weself...Tamina come in from school di edda day a talk bout Global Warmin. We sidung an watch one programme-Yuh now ow much wata it tek fi mek one T-shirt? Bout 2500 lita. 2500! LITA! Fi mek one T-shirt. One! Bet yuh any money, if people

educate demself fi know how an weh it tek fi mek dem clodes, dem would tink two time before dem buy it. Yuh know Black people spen di mos money pan clodes an beauty? Yuh know a trut me a talk. Weh dem need fi du a put it pan di label. Show ow much wata it tek fi mek it, an put one picture a di sweat shop weh dem ave di likkl pikni a stich up di garment in. Soon we cah ave wi Fish Friday b'cah di fish nyam up di whole a di scandal bag weh we dash in a di sea...Dem a fi soon change di Dance tuh Mutton Monday. Coco a guh bex!...Tamisha set up direct debit fi me fi donate mi money to charity, she did wah do one particular charity, but me tell ar seh me nah gih weh mi money fi dem fi spen pon oman, so she decide pon Complete water, Dem suppose tuh spen 100% a di public donation pon di project dem, but me a watch dem b'cah me wah know which part my money a guh...kuh pon dis, see one next yah!

Translation

Have you seen how I got to work today? There was a piece of commotion yesterday evening, I don't know what happened to Tamisha, she was on my case about the food that I'm eating, and how I don't exercise and so forth. It was the Jelly I was eating, I had to ask her which one of us is the Adult around here. She acts like she gave birth to me. She was saying she doesn't want me to die so I have to do some exercise and start eating well. She's just like her Mother, always fussing about something or another. She slapped it out of my hand! I shouted at her and told her not to treat people like that and leave me with my Jelly...I've got my bicycle out the back-Yo Jerky! Jerky! Look what I found in the Fish. look. I saw something in the mouth and when I started to gut it, I realised what it was. Nah man! This isn't right. Soon we can't eat good food because we've mashed up the bloody Ocean-Too lazy to clean up after ourselves. Tamina came in from school the other day talking about Global Warming.

We sat down and watched a programme- Do you know how much water it takes to make one T-shirt? About 2500 liters. 2500! LITERS! To make one Tshirt. One! I bet you any money, if people educated themselves to know how and what it takes to make their clothes, they would think twice before buying it. You know Black people spend the most money on clothes and beauty? You know it's the truth I'm talking about. What they need to do is put it on the label. Show how much water it takes to make it, and put a picture of the sweat shop they've got the kids stitching the garments in. Soon we won't be able to have Fish Fridays because the fish have eaten all the plastic bags which have been thrown in the sea...They're going to have to change the Dance to Mutton Mondays soon. Coco's going to be mad!...Tamisha set up a direct debit for us to donate my money to charity, she wanted to do a certain charity, but I told her that I'm not going to give them my money for them to spend it on Women, so she decided on Complete Water. They're supposed to spend 100% of public donations to the cause but I'm keeping an eye on them because I want to know where my money is going...look at this, here's another one!

Present.
Marsha is a 42 year old redskin woman. She is Mother to Dejaune. She has rough hands from the work she does. Previous to this conversation, Marsha was about to walk onto her drive to go into her home but her neighbour had just put her rubbish out and stopped Marsha in her tracks. This was a conversation Marsha didn't want to have, especially because of the weather. It's extremely cold outside hence the layers she has on. Having had a natter with her neighbour, she now stands in her living room, taking off her layers as she recites the conversation to her Husband who luxuriates on the sofa. Her home is in order and everything has a place. She and her Husband have a great relationship but one thing she knows he hates is boasting and pride. That's why she starts the conversation off so tentatively. As she stands chatting away she takes her outdoor coat, gloves, scarf and hat off. Not only does Marsha want to tell

her husband about the conversation she just had, she also wants to gloat about the fact her neighbour has praised her for her great work as a Mother. This is something that she wants her husband to participate in, which in fact, her husband is having no part in the idle gossip.

Me jus dun talk tuh Shelly...From crass di road, a number tirty tree. She a tell me bout ar son, ow im lazy an ave no ambition. Every mornin she git up fi gah work, im de in a im bed. Five o clock when she reach back, di bwoy a lay dung sed place she lef im. Not even im dutty plate weh pile up in a di sink im wash, neida run di vacume ova di ouse. She seh all im good fah a play pon im X sintin, pis, shit an nyam food, den gahn out til wat a'clock a night. She can chat ar business you si.

Me tell ar fi llow im, im soon brook outta it. She tun tuh me an ask me ow mi bwoy a duh b'cah she see im a lef out every mornin. Me tell ar Dejaun is doin very well tank you, me tell ar seh im nearly finish im aprentaship an im ave im part time job. Me even tell ar sometime when Dejaun finish work before wi, im come ome an cook one pot a food, ear ar now! Maybe im can tek Jamie unda im wing, teach im a few thingz bout life.

Now, me sure seh Dejaaun neva bread no chroublmekaJamie-A nuh im suppos tuh guide im, im ave Mada an Fada live a yard wid im, im nuh ave no brada or sista, a nuh Dejaun job fi tek care a dem pikni, dem should a bruk im from long time, me dun tell Dejaun anytime im pas im pan di street, im nuh fi mek eye contac wid im, fi corrup mi good good son, no sah! (Walks to the Kitchen, storms back out, through to the living room to the bottom of di staires) Dejaun! Come wash up di dutty plate weh yuh lef in a mi sink.

Translation

I just finished speaking to Shelly...From across the road, at number 33. She was telling me about her son, how he's lazy and has no ambition. Every

Morning when she gets up to go to work, he's in bed. When she gets back at 5 oclock, the boy's still in the same place she left him. He doesn't even wash his dirty plates that he's piled up in the sink nor does he run the Hoover over the house. She said all he's good for is playing on his x something, piss, shit and eating food, then he's gone out till whatever o'clock at night. She can talk about her business you know. I told her to give him a chance, he'll grow out of it. She turned to me and asked me how my son's doing because she sees him leave out every morning. I told her Dejaune's doing very well thank you, he's nearly finished his apprenticeship and he's got his part time job. I told her about when Dejaune finishes work before us, he cooks Dinner too, listen to what she says next! Maybe he can take Jamie under his wing, teach him a few things about life.

Now, I'm sure Dejaune didn't give birth to TroublemakerJamie-It's not him that's supposed to guide him, he's got a Mother and Father who lives at home with him, he hasn't got any Brothers or

Sisters, it's not Dejaune's job to take care of their child, they should've broken him out of that a long time ago, I've already told Dejaune whenever he passes him on the street, not to make eye contact with him. To corrupt my good son, no way.
(Walks to the Kitchen, stormes back out, through the living room to the bottom of the stairs)

Dejaune! Come and wash up the dirty plates that you've left in my sink.

Coconut

1991. Coco, 9 years old. She sells coconuts by the side of the road. People know of her and look after her in the street. She is the youngest of the (professional) Higglers who tout for trade from the passing crowds of holiday makers and citizens of the Parish. She has a patch between a shoe seller and a jewellery maker, who's work isn't worth more than its time. Not much is known about the girls family or where she actually comes from. The day is hot, very hot. The street is busy with shoppers and workers on their lunch breaks. She's wearing a light blue dress with no shoes, her hair is cainrowed in two Du Du plaits. We open to see her touting for business.

Coconut! Coconut! Everytin' Coconut. Coconut wata, fresh like yuh Daughta, one stop firs, come quench yuh tirst, Grata Cake, Coconut Drops an Gizada, is a nice likkle treat, mek yuh work arder. Coconut! Coconut! Come get yuh Coconut. Low in a

calorie, suh di celulite yuh cyar see, it ave di B vitamin an di good protein, drink all a dat, mek yuh tick an lean. Coconut, Coconut! Everybady wah di Coconut oil. Use it fi repel mosquito, cook an clean, use it pon yuh elbow dem, mek sure dem cream. Coconut, Coconut everybady need Coconut. Yuh ave it in a yuh floor mat, fishing net, mattress, an sack, it deh inside a whole heap a tings, tings weh yuh nuh even know it ave. Coconut, Coco-Yes Sir? Coconut yuh want, Coconut me ave, all kina Coconut fi mek yuh feel glad. Me sell one fi $150 or two fi $250...Hey! Excuse mi Sir! Yuh nah nuh manners? How come yuh tun yuh back an me still a converse wid yuh Sir? You look almighty glad when yuh see weh me ave, but when yuh ear di price yuh face look affright. Yuh tan up ya, an yuh shoes a shine, clean collar pan yuh shirt and yuh pants ave in line, look like yuh ave fresh cut, clean line pon yuh mustache an nuh pimple nah buss. Is di cologne me taste before me see yuh ova yonda.
A bade yuh bade in a it? Me juss a wonda. Me see yuh ave Chevrole key pan yuh keyring, a floss yuh a

floss or yuh ave di real ting? Eida way it nuh look right fi yuh fi come ova an jus pass by. Does one are two Coconut sweet yuh?-An it alright, yuh can pay fi it wid di Twenty Dolla...But me don't ave nuh change fi it, suh tanks fi olla.

(To herself)

Ow a genklman nice suh, come give me big big tip. Me a guh eat good a fish Friday tonight!...Coconut! Coconut! Everybady ave Coconut.

Translation

Coconut! Coconut! Everything's Coconut. Coconut Water, fresh like your Daughter, stop here first, come and quench your thirst, Grater Cake, Coconut Drops and Gizzada, it's a nice little treat, makes you work harder. Coconut! Coconut! Come and get your Coconuts. Low in calories, so the celulite you can't see, it's got the B Vitamin and the good Proteins, drink all of that, it'll make you tick and lean.

Coconut! Coconut! Everybody wants the Coconut oil. Use it to repel Mosquitos, cook and clean, use it on your elbows, make sure they are
creamed.
Coconut, Coconut! Everybody needs Coconut
You've got it in your floor mat, fishing net, mattress and sack, it's inside of a whole heap of things, things that you don't even know it has. Coconut, Coco-Yes Sir? Coconut you want Coconuts I have, all sorts of Coconuts to make you feel glad. I sell One for $150 or Two for $250...Hey! Excuse me Sir! Haven't you got any manners? Why have you turned your back on me and I'm still conversing with you Sir?
You looked almighty glad when you saw what I had, but when you heard the price your face looked affright. You're standing here and your shoes are shining, a clean collar on your shirt and your trousers have a line in, it looks like you have a fresh cut, clean line on your moustache and no spots have bust. It's the cologne I tasted before I saw you over there. Did you have a bath in it? I'm just wondering.

I see you have a Chevrolet key on your keyring, is it boast your boasting or do you have the real thing? Either way it doesn't look right for you to come over and just pass by. Would you like one or two Coconuts?-And it's alright, you can pay for it with the Twenty Dollars...But I don't have any change for it, so thanks for hollering.

(To herself)

How's that gentleman so nice, he gave me such a big tip. I'm going to eat well at fish Fridays tonight! Coconut! Coconut! Everybody has Coconut.

BE KIND, WALK GOOD.

Printed in Great Britain
by Amazon

60879328R00092